years i walked at your side

years i walked at your side

Selected Poems by

Mordechai Geldman

Translated by

Tsipi Keller

excelsior editions
AN IMPRINT OF STATE UNIVERSITY OF NEW YORK PRESS

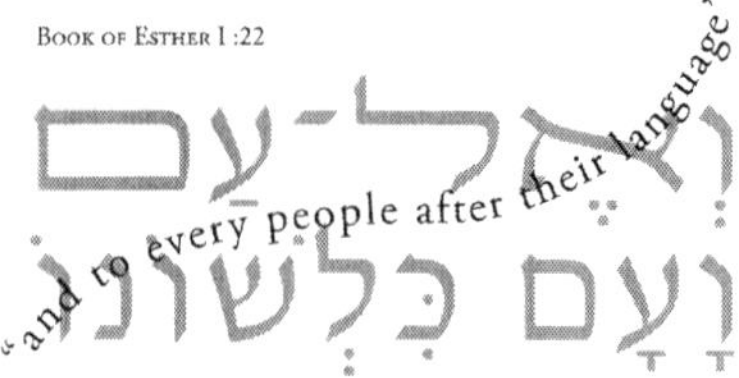

Published with the support of The Institute for the Translation of Hebrew Literature, Israel, and Consulate General of Israel in New York

Cover art: Semadar Megged

Published by State University of New York Press

Printed in the United States of America

Excelsior Editions is an imprint of State University of New York Press

For information, contact State University of New York Press, Albany, NY
www.sunypress.edu

Library of Congress Cataloging-in-Publication Data

Names: Geldmann, Mordechay, 1946- author. | Keller, Tsipi translator.
Title: Years I walked at your side : selected poems / Mordechai Geldman ; selected and translated from the Hebrew by Tsipi Keller ; introduction by Tsipi Keller and Ruth Kartun-Blum.
Description: Albany : State University of New York Press, 2018. | Series: Excelsior editions | Includes index.
Identifiers: LCCN 2018000363| ISBN 9781438472386 (pbk. : alk. paper) | ISBN 9781438472393 (e-book)
Classification: LCC PJ5054.G393 A2 2018 | DDC 892.41/6—dc23 LC record available at https://lccn.loc.gov/2018000363

10 9 8 7 6 5 4 3 2 1

contents

from *Tamir's Poems* (2007)

years i walked at your side

Selected Poems by

Mordechai Geldman

Translated by

Tsipi Keller

excelsior editions

AN IMPRINT OF STATE UNIVERSITY OF NEW YORK PRESS

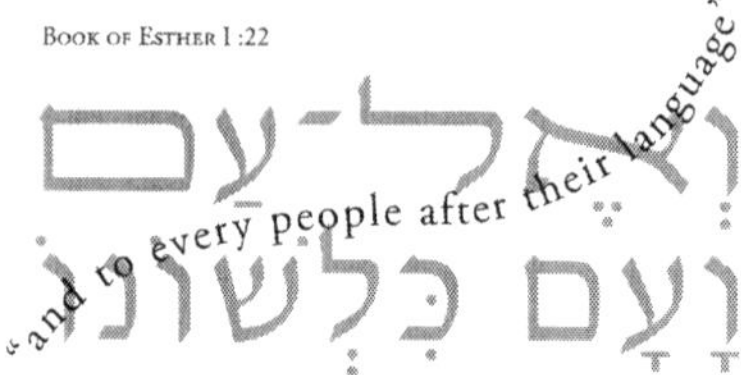

Published with the support of The Institute for the Translation of Hebrew Literature, Israel, and Consulate General of Israel in New York

Cover art: Semadar Megged

Published by State University of New York Press

Published by arrangement with The Institute for the Translation of Hebrew Literature

Printed in the United States of America

Excelsior Editions is an imprint of State University of New York Press

For information, contact State University of New York Press, Albany, NY
www.sunypress.edu

Library of Congress Cataloging-in-Publication Data

Names: Geldmann, Mordechay, 1946- author. | Keller, Tsipi translator.
Title: Years I walked at your side : selected poems / Mordechai Geldman ; selected and translated from the Hebrew by Tsipi Keller ; introduction by Tsipi Keller and Ruth Kartun-Blum.
Description: Albany : State University of New York Press, 2018. | Series: Excelsior editions | Includes index.
Identifiers: LCCN 2018000363| ISBN 9781438472386 (pbk. : alk. paper) | ISBN 9781438472393 (e-book)
Classification: LCC PJ5054.G393 A2 2018 | DDC 892.41/6—dc23 LC record available at https://lccn.loc.gov/2018000363

10 9 8 7 6 5 4 3 2 1

contents

from *Tamir's Poems* (2007)

from *Poem of the Heart* (2004)

from *Oh My Dear Wall* (2000)

from *Book of Ask* (1997)

from *Eye* (1993)

from *Milano* (1988)

introduction

"Be plural like the universe!"
—Fernando Pessoa

Mordechai Geldman came of age as a poet in the seventies, a heady and auspicious time in the development of modern Hebrew poetry. Young poets such as Yair Hurwitz and Yona Wallach—friends and contemporaries of Geldman with whom he shared a strong affinity—were publishing their first books, inspired by and benefitting from the freedoms their elders had established. These poets—David Avidan, Natan Zach, Yehuda Amichai, and Dahlia Ravikovitch—who began publishing two decades earlier, had turned away from the poetic conventions of their immediate predecessors, notably Natan Alterman and Avraham Shlonsky, who were still very dominant in the fifties and sixties. Avidan, Zach, and their contemporaries vehemently rejected the flowery, the hyperbolic, and the sentimental, along with rhyme and formal verse. They advocated for and embraced the modernism of Ezra Pound, T. S. Eliot, W. H. Auden, and Wallace Stevens, to name a few, and so paved the way for Geldman and his generation.

In addition to the revitalization of language, the modernist poets also had to engage and reclaim the self. The prominent poets of the previous generations had adopted the persona of prophet-poet, "bearing an enormous weight of national responsibility,"* whereas their successors shed collective responsibility and placed their focus on the individual.

If Geldman's early poems tended toward the surreal, relying on linguistic exploration and wizardry, his vision soon turned inward, as Geldman more and

* Aminadav Dykman. Introduction to *Poets on the Edge: An Anthology of Contemporary Hebrew Poetry* (SUNY Press, 2008).

more came to favor the simple, the true, the authentic. Initially, he was inspired primarily by Rilke; later, such poets as Czesław Milosz, Zbigniew Herbert, Eliot, and Stevens were also instrumental in reshaping his poetic sensibilities. The translator and poet Rina Litvin said of his work, "One of Geldman's poetic characteristics is the arc of his cultural associations and sensibilities. . . . The sensual and cultural richness, the fine musicality, the originality of observation, and the thematic singularity combine to make Geldman's work an important and beautiful treasure in contemporary Hebrew poetry."

To date, Geldman has published fourteen volumes of poetry and five essay collections. He has received every major poetry prize, including the Bialik Life Achievement Prize in Poetry (2010). The poems presented here are drawn from his two-volume *Collected Poems: Years I Walked at Your Side*, published by Hakibbutz Hameuchad Publishing House and the Bialik Institute in 2010–11. The Hebrew edition begins with New Poems (2010) and goes back in time till 1970; this edition also begins with 2010 and goes back in time to 1988.

The first poem in *Collected Poems*, "Voice," begins:

> What is his true voice?
>
> Have words enfolded him
> in murmurs
> in forms
> in worn-out patterns that came before him?

A practicing clinical psychologist, a student of Kabbalah and Zen Buddhism, it seems natural for a poet like Geldman to open with a question. A question or doubt begets another: Nothing is taken for granted, not even such basic notions as one's voice and identity. Geldman's act of questioning allows for the complex development and examination of differing aspects of an issue and ultimately leads to revelation and creation. Explorative, yet without ever being dogmatic or aiming for any one "logical" conclusion, Geldman frequently surprises with the turns he takes. The second stanza informs us:

"Person" described him
better than "frog"
but the croaking of frogs in the night's ponds
or the whistle of birds at dusk
or the sound of fruit dropping to the ground
drew him out better than Hebrew
as Being revealed itself to him in its fullness

The evocation of sound—"the croaking of frogs or . . . the sound of fruit dropping to the ground"—brings about a mystical stirring in a way that language alone cannot. Equally stirring, later in the poem, are "Yiddish melodies"—"songs of mournful wisdoms" from the past—evoking a history of dispossession and suffering, both personal and cultural. Many of Geldman's generation grew up with such melodies, frequently sung by mothers homesick for family members, for a landscape, for a way of life that was now lost to them. The poem continues for six more stanzas, leading poet and reader in an ever-widening circle. Here, as elsewhere, the long breath suits Geldman's slow, careful, meditative tempo; the son of Holocaust survivors, collective memories cling to him. And in his poem "Spring," he takes us back to "a city in ruins," to Munich after the war; to a time he may remember mainly from his parents' stories; to a time when

horrific sights huddled in the streets
refusing to sink in the gutter of oblivion
....
American soldiers with glinting teeth were the messengers of purity
German women famished and sallow copulated with able-bodied
 blacks
Jews from the camps went back to commerce
and put flesh on their bones

Geldman himself is a survivor of sorts. In the cycle "Home Poems" he describes himself as "the only son of nomads," repeatedly banished from their homes,

whose last homes
were burnt by homicidal platoons, officers of death
who decreed new lodgings for them:
convict huts, mass graves, heaps of ashes, chimneys,
tunnels, cellars, gutters, the thick of forests

Moody, authoritative, and oftentimes ironic, the poet straddles multiple modes of being, epitomizing the dual facets of the artist: on the one hand, he is an individual living his personal life and, on the other, he is a messenger from the beyond, engaged in an impersonal creative process. One gets the sense that Geldman is an intensely private person and yet is compelled to reveal areas of vulnerability, weakness, and hurt. As he explains in his preface, he discovered early on that poetry suited his need to "reveal and conceal" himself at the same time. He also discovered that through language he can recreate himself as an unconstrained being in a fanciful universe that serves as a temporary hideout. In "Rivers," he finds sanctuary as "a water child":

Our dinghy sailed upon sweet waters
that flowed pure from a wondrous source
father paddled the oars
mother shuddered with the dinghy's jolts
....
I became a water child
an orphan living in the depths of the river
with the other water kids
among intelligent and silent fish
amazing daffodils

Similarly, in "Home Poems" he builds himself a home in a massive ficus tree where "birds were my mother and father / chicks were my brothers / an ant became my cousin."

In addition to his work as a poet, Geldman is also an art critic and essayist, and his poems frequently include themes from and references to classical mythology, while also echoing the roots he sprang from. Growing up in a religious environment, he assimilated the power contained in speech through the study of the Torah and Talmud, through the exercise of *pilpul* (disputation), and through the act of memorizing the daily recitation of prayer and verses from *Tehillim* (Psalms)—all poetic forms in themselves. And even though he no longer practices Orthodox Judaism, his language is a conflation of the old and new, inflected by biblical cadences, alongside the vernacular and colloquial. In the words of Uzi Shavit: "The clarity and virtuosity of [Geldman's] language, its musicality, grant a classicist dimension to his natural non-conformism, as he engages the darker corners of human existence."

His poems, invariably, are a journey, both physical and internal, as they touch on a wide variety of issues and preoccupations ranging from the petty, everyday incidents, such as a female passenger on a bus trying to peek into his notebook, to sudden, if brief, realizations of harmony and alignment with the sublime; from a murder in his quiet neighborhood, to reflections upon the fleeting and the eternal; from Socratic ideals of love for truth and beauty, to the reality of anonymous sex. The poem "At Your Side" begins as an introspective, nearly metaphysical, disquisition, but soon plunges into a seedy nightclub where

> the G-string girls
> are blind dolls
> hollow Hebrew dolls
> hungry and hunger-inducing
> ....
> ticking beauties
> like an explosive shaheeda*
> tinkling cunts
> in a chill-out trance

Routinely solitary, whether on foot or on his bike, Geldman is a tourist in his own town; Tel Aviv, especially his neighborhood near Kikar Milano, plays an important role in the poems. Particularly prominent is Nahal Ha'Yarkon, a river near his home that, over the years, has been transformed from a polluted,

* In Arabic, female martyr

neglected area into a park where the poet finds access to the unseen and to the incessant flow of the mind, leading to epiphanies such as:

*

All at once
with no preparation or intent on my part
the ocean of infinity was revealed

The play of lights
on the dark water of the neighborhood river
the hum of distant roads
spilling into the empty lilac of the horizon
the jittery waves in the soft alien sea
into which the river flows—
all spoke of its presence

I did not ask to be lost in it
and I did not fear to exist in it
as a tiny speck

With lucid delight
I perceived the blind giant
in whose palm the planet spun
and I mulled over my mystifying ability
to overlook day after day
his immense presence

Geldman's poetic journey is transformative, and he exhorts us to pay attention, to be *mindful*, and perhaps share in the kabbalists' vision that "There can be no perfecting above without the perfecting influence of humans when they are righteous and act from love" (Zohar 2:155a). Expansion and transformation of the self are paramount in his work, as is the need for beauty and love. For Geldman, one of the first openly gay poets of his generation, physical beauty and its consort, sexual attraction, is the nexus of exaltation and pain. Beautiful forms attract him, not only on the physical plane but also on the spiritual plane. In "Form" he tells us:

> All he ever wanted was a form—
> at times it was revealed to him in boys
> at times in paintings
> in old ruins or poems
> and at times even in frogs or birds
> in other words a living breathing form
> ....
> He sought after his form
> like one fleeing formlessness
> he sought after his form
> with great desperation
> he sought after a form
> that would be admired by all
> because his parents his progenitors
> had willed his excellent form
> because the form of his parents
> had been broken by polished officers of murder
> who murdered even their own god

When the poet turns sixty, he sees a naked skull in the mirror and is frightened. But

> against the gaping void
> your slender dark silhouette suddenly appeared
> stirring in me such a powerful passion
> ....
> but something impenetrable in your nature—
> a strange and alien charm
> a psychopathic Eros a cruel temptation
> entrapped my consciousness in your illusion
> ....

you became the denied love
the love denied me beforehand as ever
from the moment of my birth
and I with a queer tenacity
set out on a last battle to conquer it
in your boyish immature heart

"Sixty" is from Geldman's 2007 collection, *Tamir's Poems*, a book-length cycle of love poems inspired by the twelfth-century Sufi mystic Rumi's love poems for Shams, *The Works of Shams of Tabriz*. Geldman wrote most of *Tamir's Poems* in Anatalia, Turkey, not far from Konya, where Rumi is buried. In "True Compassion" the older poet addresses his young lover Tamir directly, again reflecting on his own mortality:

You probably won't believe this
but when my love for you first flared up
I considered above all how you would handle my corpse
when my time came

Although habitually alone in his poems, Geldman is not a recluse. We also find him in cafés, bookstores, clothing stores, the post office, the gym. Cell phones, favorite ringtones, and texting get their due, including in a twenty-two-poem sequence entitled "Text Messaging Poems." Sometimes his neighbors invade his poems ("Abused Neighbor"), and other times, assuming a different persona, he invades their homes, if only in his imagination ("Dolinger"). In "Dolinger," the eponymous figure "grew to hate/the life of a single poet," preferring, for a change, to contemplate, in the home of his neighbors,

coitus kindled by scant desire
electronic gadgets collecting in the kitchen
defrosted Chinese dinners
eaten quickly in front of a flickering rectangle

In conjunction with a sharp intellect, a thread of compassion runs through the poems, embracing the weak, the voiceless, the foreign—sometimes illegal—migrant worker. Humor is also present, especially in his poems about cats, dogs, birds, even flies and mosquitoes. A most affecting and witty poem, "Chu," is about his beloved cat, who was run over by a car:

> The cat Chu like most of the cats in our land
> was a fourth-world citizen
> living at the bottom of society's ladder
> ....
> But I raised him from the gutter
> to be a domestic noble tiger
> a green-eyed striped tiger
> daintily stepping on pillows and armchairs
> feeding on Italian preserves
> and choosing to catnap with his head in my palm
> ....
> At night Chu came to me in his spirit
> and said in the language of humans:
> "Now that you've written two poems
> you're ready to forget me
> but I'm a cat of three poems
> if not more"

Geldman tells us in his preface, "My poetry comes from the inner void that meditation creates." In kabbalistic tradition God had to contract himself (*tsimtsum*) to make room for His creation, and the poet, too, "empties" himself to make room for the poem. And just as God used language in the act of creation ("Let there be light"), so does the poet. For Geldman, the determination to seek and to understand through the act of writing is equated with the determination to live. To feel and to formulate becomes not only a way of life but a survival strategy. The devotion to the written word is sacramental and binding, impelling him toward precision, on the one hand, and toward humility, on the other. The long, seminal poem "At Your Side," whose first line is the title of this volume, begins meditatively, biblically, addressing someone specific who yet remains unnamed, addressing God, and addressing all of us:

Years I walked at your side
like our prophet Isaiah
barefoot naked and bare
I will put on no cover
until you see me
until you recognize an other
one person
at least
and so know yourself as well
no need for you to come
to a Jerusalem submerged
in the depths of the ocean
I'd be content if you reached into your heart
the heart within your heart
I'd be content with innocence lost
with a white lamb
grazing in the brilliant green
of budding wheat

— *Tsipi Keller and Ruth Kartun-Blum*

I Wrote Write Will Write

Author's Preface to the Hebrew Edition of the Two-Volume *Collected Poems: Years I Walked at Your Side*

When I was four or five years old, my parents put me in a wooden playpen and left the house for a short while. I was alone. It was during Chanukah, and somehow I was able to reach for the box of candles in the room. Using a few candles, I "wrote" my name on the sheet. Wishing my parents to see what I had done, I curled up in the corner of the playpen and waited. As to the color of the candles I picked, my memory offers two versions: in one, they're red and blue; in the other, yellow.

It is possible that this "installation" is the very first poem I wrote, a poem of two words, made with cylinders of colored wax. I recalled this event ten years or so ago, and came to see it as a sort of preamble to my work as a poet.

In this "poem" we may perceive several mental elements that developed over time: love for light; an affinity for the sacred; a penchant for the miraculous and the wondrous; a keen dialectic stance toward Jewish identity (the Chanukah story, after all, also includes the Greeks); conflicting proclivities (self-contained vs. outgoing); and self-reliance after the departure of a loved one.

But the first real poem I ever wrote was in a notebook when I was fourteen years old and sitting on the edge of a white bathtub. During my tenth or eleventh year, at a golden noon-hour of the Sabbath, my mother sat on the edge of the tub and cut her wrist with a razor blade. When I walked in on her, she quickly hid her hand behind her back, and drops of blood trickled onto the tub. I took fright as one pulled by a big wave into the depths of the sea. I may have screamed; I may have yelled at her. She allowed me to bandage her wrist, and then she went to bed. When evening came, she received our guests pleasantly and lucidly. She was particularly beautiful that evening, and a soft pale light radiated from her face.

My young mind interpreted this as an attempt to kill herself. And yet, it is clear she did not intend to end her life that Saturday noon, for we were all in the house, and it was highly unlikely we would not catch her in the act. This suicide spectacle was a call for help and, possibly, an attempt to tighten her hold on the family. Whatever the case, the immediate impact was very traumatic to my soul, and from then on, for many years, I lived with the anxiety that she would kill herself. The razor blade, the kind no longer manufactured, became for me a thin, tiny steel door to an apocalyptic world. When my parents' quarrels escalated, I hid the blades in secret places, and maybe that's why, when she tried again, she chose sleeping pills. The Hypnos pills, too, she swallowed when we were all in the house—my father, my sister, and I—and night had already fallen on Tel Aviv.

I crossed the night air, running to the house of Dr. Goldberg with the urgency of one whose mother's life depended on him. Wind shrieked in my ears, even though no wind was blowing. The doctor lived in our neighborhood, and I summoned him around midnight. He arrived without delay, flushed out her stomach, and didn't send her to the hospital.

I recall my mother's suicide attempts vividly, but the memory of myself sitting on the edge of the white enamel tub and writing my first poem rouses my suspicion. Is this how it actually happened, or did my imagination make up this "memory"? Still, such a creation of the imagination, demanding for itself the status of an actual memory, surely carries a strong emotional significance.

I believe that the edge of the tub functions in this memory as a border between life and death, and the writing functions as both an act of suicide and of revival. The trope of my mother's suicides can be interpreted in this recollection as a sick and desperate attempt to speak her silence, to reveal in a scream all the pain that has accumulated in her. When a speaking self speaking its selfhood is missing, or when an adequate listener to the soul is missing, life is not worth living. Writing the poem on the edge of the tub was an attempt to make the subject speak from the depths of its subjectivity.

Correspondingly, as time passes, I understand that in choosing poetry, in choosing the identity of a poet, there was also a suicidal element. Sailing in the rough sea of life to wherever the wind may take me, the pen of the poet my only navigation tool, is, in my view, an "extreme" adventure, very much like the daredevil stunts of bikers, or the challenge of whitewater rafting, that often entail a suicidal element.

It is also possible to view the poet's adventure—a poet who began his poetic "career" because of the circumstance of his mother's potential suicide—as a descent into hell, very much like that of Orpheus, the archetypical poet. From this aspect, the razor blade or the edge of the tub were the gates of hell the poet sought in order to re-find his mother who was lost in her suicide attempt, lost to herself and to her son, even if she did not die. I hope the reader will not judge me pretentious when I compare my case to that of Orpheus, but will read instead my willingness to humbly recognize the influence archetypal patterns exert on all of us.

At any rate, in my conscious experience, the choice of the poet's pen carried with it the awareness of my natural alienation that came with the need to differentiate myself from my mother and her tragedy. She imposed her soul on her son with exceptional force, and the separation from her became essential. Eventually, I began to cultivate the alienation that the differentiation wrought, in order to afford myself the utmost spiritual freedom, even as this involved a great fall from the sacred boundaries of faith that keep its members within the established order. Additionally, the stance of estrangement allowed me to create and recreate myself as an observing, reflecting, poetic self. The suicide of the self as predefined by its circumstances allows the self to be born and reborn anew. The one who finds himself is lost, and the lost is already found. Thus spoke another suicide, who knew well that Jerusalem kills its prophets: Jesus the Galilean.

It is possible that by sitting on the white enamel and writing a poem, I told my mother: I can live without you, because I'll give birth to myself again by writing. And also: I will save myself from your fate because I'll do what you couldn't do: give expression to myself, write myself. And also: If you thought that I would live by your soul alone—here I am creating my own soul against your being that threatens to silence it. And also: You love poetry, poems always revived you, so here, let me write a poem for you, and please don't leave me, don't part from me, don't spill your blood. And also: Like you, I'll commit suicide, and, like you, I'll live again. When evening comes, I'll be reborn and will receive my guests with a solemn, radiant calm, singing for them a little song.

There are several reasons why I devoted myself to writing poetry, and I'll point out the most compelling three. The first and oldest, which goes back to my childhood, was experiencing my mother's egocentric and demanding love, allowing me no room to exist as a subject. She loved a virtual child—created by her desires, her dreams, her anxieties—and not the actual child. The actual child experienced breadths of desire, pain, and fear that were denied in the communication between himself and his mother; writing allowed my secret self to exist and to express itself while continuing to hide. Poetry is the art of revelation by code. Poetry reveals and conceals at the same time.

My struggle against my mother's tyrannical and demanding love also made me especially sensitive to the sway of groups and institutions, and I soon broke away from the religious structure I grew up in. Wherever I went, I always sought to guard my freedom and individuality. The stance of the observing alien, so characteristic of poets, became my preferred mode. This identity served me as an instrument for self-expression against all the communal forces that tried to mold me. A childish intuition kept whispering in my ear that I'm surrounded by lies and fabricated images, that the only undeniable truth was the fact that my parents arrived in Israel from the valley of death. With the identity of the estranged, the alien, the other, I could construct my individuality, a point of view unique to me. Poetry was the main catalyst in my individuation; I created my poetry, and my poetry created me. Still, my work as a psychologist contributed as well.

As I matured and my identity took shape, my gaze shifted from the self—from seeking expression and definition to very important narcissistic needs—to a reality that is revealed when the interests and structures of the self are kept in check. My focus on Zen Buddhism, Buddhism, and Patanjali Yoga, turned experience from a state of emptiness to an occurrence most desired and formative. Poetry became the means to express the experiencing self that has managed to restrain its selfhood and halted the a priori patterns that stifled it. My poetry issues from the inner void that meditation creates. I've cultivated in myself the negative capability that Keats saw as the source of Shakespeare's poetry.

I believed that, like everyone else, I saw very little because of the a priori patterns dictating my experiences—I didn't see myself, nor the other, nor the landscape, nor the circumstances that ruled me, since my sight functioned according to its habits of seeing and not the actual. But I could strive to empty my consciousness from my habitual self, and so allow for illuminations that would reveal the actual in relative clarity, if only for a split second. And this indeed happened. Such epiphanic events are nearly always accompanied not only with an "Ah" moment but also with a poem that comes forth as if from nowhere. You go past a field every day, every evening, you go past as if blind, until suddenly you behold it in all its *suchness*. This is a moment of redemption for you and the field. And this is also the moment of the poem.

From the start, from early childhood, I was predisposed to be overwhelmed by beauty, and this, I believe, was the driving force that compelled me to pursue poetry and art. In my childhood, the beauty of nature, people, garments, paintings, sculptures, music—all generated exhilaration and enchantment. The beautiful cast on me a strange magic and roused in me an inexplicable erotic fever. But the beautiful was also in words, perhaps even primarily in words. As a child who received a religious education, my head was filled with the sound of beautiful and holy psalms and verses from the Bible, the prayer book, and medieval poetry, as well as graceful lines from Bialik's poetry for children. I, too, wished to create such beautiful verse. Over time, my poetry favored the "truthful" and the "good," and gradually rejected that which employed aestheticism only, charm for the sake of charming. But the ideal of a verse that holds a mysterious power to imprint itself in your brain forever still speaks to my heart.

from

New Poems

(2010)

Voice

What is his true voice?

Have words enfolded him
in murmurs
in forms
in worn-out patterns that came before him?

"Person" described him
better than "frog"
but the croaking of frogs in the night's ponds
or the whistle of birds at dusk
or the sound of fruit dropping to the ground
drew him out better than Hebrew
as Being revealed itself to him in its fullness

And at moments of involuntary openness
when fatigue dissolved his inhibitions
Yiddish melodies floated up in his mind
songs of mournful wisdoms
of a cursed chosen people of God
tunes of an exiled truth and suffering
and the rolling of the dead*

---

* Refers to the belief that when the Messiah arrives, Jews who had died in the Diaspora would roll under their graves, through tunnels and caves, to Israel for the Resurrection

And at times other voices
voices of others
sneaked surreptitiously into his secret cave
echoed in his voice and from within
infecting his voice with alienation
alien voices echoed in his voice simulating his voice
his voice at times getting lost in simulation

But was it really simulation
was there really a voice that was not his voice
as it used his mouth his palate his tongue his teeth
in order to set forth in the world
out into a vastness of odd-looking funnels

And wasn't his voice muddled up
when adjusted to the auditory frequency of listeners
who had no intention to listen
and certainly never made the effort
and in fact never could

A suspicion rippled through him
annulling any pure sound
true like the roar of a river
virginal like the note of a reed
that has just been pulled from the edge of the swamp
or cruel and desirous like the wail of prairie wolves

But always an intense pain
an absolute final truth
whose voice was a scream or a shout
a voice distilled of dross
a voice of pure pain
pure voice of pain
four final words
and the song of wasps
in landfills

Poems from Amirim

NOCTURNAL WIND

Winds clamored in forests
until they stormed like ocean breakers
and when stillness surfaced from the bottom
a puppy tried its voice

I who lay on my back in the dark
utterly impoverished
witnessed his existence

VASTNESS

When trees gently rustle
I exist in my familiar size
when trees erupt like the sea
I contract to the size of an ant or a leaf
the wind that gusts among the trees
asserts that we belong in the universe among galaxies
and the widening vastness is a wily witness

Amirim is a vegetarian moshav in Upper Galilee.

CAROB IN BLOOM

Its branches a crisscross composite
a grid of leaves flowers and bees
this is the dome of the temple
its scent a hormonal incense
wherein bees murmur prayers
anyone fearing his own passion
must not enter this temple
must not offer prayer to the goddess of fertility
in the company of heathen bees

FULL MOON

A slender chaste virginal moon
was born this evening at the edge of the sky
trembling like a bashful Muslim boy
yet it is not tonight's moon
since a full moon
floats like a looking glass upon the dark valleys
its form born of my soul
and its glow

SPIRITUALITY

The spirit of the mountains teaches spirituality

When the roar of the excited wind
arrives from its vast distances like a tidal wave
you comprehend the entity awaiting
beyond the woods
beyond yourself
the wind of the mountains teaches a magnitude
that has no measure

THE ANEMONE FLOWER

The anemone burns immodestly
forget yourself
she demands
look into the eye in the heart of the fire
into the hole
into the peephole
peep into the beyond of your self
behold the mountain of crossways

The anemone burns immodestly
even though winter is still far away
and the anemone and cyclamen have yet to bud

Missing (1)

A notice with the heading “Missing”
bearing the image of an elderly man in a suit
was posted on fences and trees in our neighborhood
“Left his home on February 3, 2005
and hasn’t been seen since.”

If he eloped with his beloved to Malta
choosing a few days of happiness
over death in life in the bosom of his family
it is clear he would never be found

But if he chose fields of spring
and he makes his way beyond the horizon
until he tires of walking
he would lie among flowers and ants

Then dogs would find him
a crow poking his eyes
and a mouse gnawing his fingers

Missing (2)

A notice with the heading "Missing"
posted on fences by his relatives
and bearing the image of an elderly man in a suit
draws me like a magnet—
do I wish to be missing now
to vanish from the world of friends and acquaintances
and become a speculation, a nagging memory, a concern, a heartache,
a thing that was lost or is hiding
waiting for his trackers
like an Assyrian tablet?

And yet it is possible it is not a wish
but the revelation of actual fact
I've been missing for days
and it's time I set out on a search
for days I've been too familiar
to myself and to others
and so have been missing from hearts
from my heart, from theirs,
the exposed covered the hidden
the known the unknown
the conscious the unconscious
the open is shut
the shut is open

I must return like a blossoming almond tree
or like a torrential rainstorm
but I may be denied

Who Do You Think You Are

As I stopped at the traffic light
a female passerby shouted at me
"Who do you think you are?"
I did not roll up the window
but having glimpsed my face she turned and went
without further arguments or insults
because I was and am no longer
and I will yet be and not be
and as to "Who do you *think* you are"
I have no answer
but I am near to knowing who I am
and an hour before my demise all will be absolutely clear
unless I sink in denials
and yet she saw compassion as well
since the temper that agitated in her
to annul me and everything else
denoted especially evil forces
that threatened that morning
every remnant of goodness
still remaining in her soul

On that cruel morning
toward the car's window
rushed a woman whose fate it was
to offer me a poem from a pit or a swamp

Loss

Something in me obsessively repeats
that I may have lost something
or left it behind
in the café or the bookstore
I had visited.
I looked everywhere
and no loss was found
nor did I discover what had been lost
but the loss
kept asserting its existence
through palpitations and minor fits.
Athenian sophists philosophized:
"A thing you haven't lost
is necessarily in your possession
you haven't lost a tail—therefore, you have a tail
or vice versa,
what you have lost was necessarily yours"
but what have I lost?
I must look for my loss
in order to know what I'm looking for
is it an object, a thing, or the thing
and was it mine before it was lost
or is it an inner authority
trying to bequeath me, like a Hellenistic sophist,
something I had never possessed
as for instance a chance
as if I ever stood a chance

Carob

"And this, by the way, is a carob tree"
said the mother to the child she held by the hand

He was about five
and she certainly didn't tell him
"The blossoms of the carob smell like sperm
and this, by the way, is a carob tree."
Mothers don't discuss sperm with their sons
and certainly not with young ones
and neither did she speak
a phrase beyond his comprehension:
"A carob in bloom
is never a dead carob
and this, by the way, is a carob tree"
but she may have pointed out to him
the names of the plants in the yard
and then the names of the trees on the street
"This is a rose tree, this a plumeria, this a crimson
and this, by the way, is a carob tree."

Yet the tree was not a carob
she deposited an error in the kid's mind
and planted an error in my mind
from which this poem is sprouting
City Hall did some planting on our street
we believed would be flower trees
but discovered barren trees
yielding tiny hard fruit
no flowers no carobs

we will therefore make do with their green shade
that will do us good during the hot summer
and we will cherish the memory of the year
when we looked forward with great anticipation
to the splendor of spring flowers
that will never flower
we will cherish the memory of our hope
that was willing to make do with flowers
relinquishing fruit
never demanding carobs
and so lacking for nothing

*

I had a revelation
at the Superstore in the mall
I was trying on a Polo shirt
of an apple-green hue
and between the two mirrors
I saw my face
and my exposed chest
and it occurred to me that I am ripening
and that soon I will drop like an apple
and will crash onto the warm ground
with an audible thump

And the earth will not shake
and the sea will not flood
and the sun and moon will not go dark

The body

An athletic body smooth and brown
its skin glowing like a wet plum
its muscles firm and lithe
is now the object of my desire
as I get older and the hour is near
so grows my lust for such a body
the more my body declines
the more my fancy cleaves to it
sublime like a reluctant god
the more absent it is
the more the soul longs for it
refusing to wear
the wrinkled mottled skin
old age granted it
the dangerously foolish soul
will not submit to the inevitable
choosing the luster of skin over the light

I Don't Know

I don't know
what I will be singing at the end
and if I will be singing at the end
I don't know
what I will be missing at the end
and if I'll be missing
to myself or to others
in the short or long term
I recall the bench—
I sit in a bright friendly sun
and watch the birds of the river
plunge in for the catch
or I witness on the next bench
two strangers touch
for the first time
and desire rises like a wave
inflaming the skin
or the first ever taste of wine
the first moments of anything at all
the virginity of life
something that holds quantities of future
now that the word future
wanes in a slow fadeout
on a movie screen

Mangs

To sleep in my arms now
only to sleep in my arms
to sleep and not to fuck
and while I labor over our dinner in the kitchen
you're sleeping in my bed
dark and skinny on a sky-blue sheet
an African Giacometti
that miraculously survived a consuming blaze

The tiring summer heat,
the quarrel between us,
as you worried, rightly, that you'd become a bottom,
this too was tiring
and in your soul I've become a new mother
a white mother, well-off, a home owner, and a cook to boot,
whose archetypical delirious phallus contains
a white treasure bearing the scent of carob blossoms
and whose arms are a provisional refuge
from the hardships of summer and life

And I in the meantime fell in love
with your odd African odor
which holds all the movies about Africa
and your weariness contracts my heart
as I plot to become your sex slave
when you wake

Mangs is the Tigrinya name of a refugee from Eritrea (author's note).

Tattoo

Across from me on the bus
sits a handsome dude
a Japanese letter tattooed on his neck

Why don't you get a tattoo as well
says my brain
a dragon or a seagull or a unicorn
will endow you with a sexy youthful look
even though it is rather late

And perhaps you're tattooed already
my brain continues
a secret tattoo
all-seeing yet invisible
which at one time was commonplace in your family
a row of blue digits
a number on the extermination line

For, on this summer morning
you are on the extermination line
considering your age
your state of mind

And a conciliatory thought comes—
it is the cell phone number of a lover,
long lost in his distances,
carved on my shoulder, on my arm,
on the tablet of my heart

At Your Side

Years I walked at your side
like our prophet Isaiah*
barefoot naked and bare
I will put on no cover
until you see me
until you recognize an other
one person
at least
and so know yourself as well
no need for you to come
to a Jerusalem submerged
in the depths of the ocean
I'd be content if you reached into your heart
the heart within your heart
I'd be content with innocence lost
with a white lamb
grazing in the brilliant green
of budding wheat

The G-string girls
play the guitar
wearing stiletto heels
the G-string girls
are blind dolls
hollow Hebrew dolls
hungry and hunger-inducing
full and empty

---

* "And the Lord said, Like as my servant Isaiah hath walked naked and barefoot three years." Isaiah 20:3 (footnote in the original).

led by strings
hobbling on heels
nails scraping
heels strumming
ticking beauties
like explosive shaheedas
tinkling cunts
in a chill-out trance

Lonely I lay on my right side
for years
now I will lie on my left
and like our prophet Ezekiel
will consume all the dung*
that's been accumulating all around
bread smeared with dung
is my daily bread
I who chose to speak
sing so you will see me
so you will see for once in your life
one person
at least one
so you will know yourself
from me and in me
so you will reach the gates of your heart

But I'll admit
everything may become messy
the river of poetry flows
the currents of change stir
the infinite is fully present

---

* "And thou shalt eat it as barley cakes, and thou shalt bake it with dung that cometh out of man, in their sight." Ezekiel 4:12 (footnote in the original).

the seer is not seen
the seen is not the seer
everything will always become messy
because the infinite
will strike you
from within the framework of your life
like a terrible angel
every angel is terrible

And when the motion of body-soul
is clearly seen
from the initial suffering
until the pain at the end
when at the light of dusk
or the light of a skull moon
the final of finals
the infinity of final
will be revealed
we will be both deserving of mercy
and we will have one heart
that will glow in the dark
in a yellow fluorescent light

The mango boys
do the tango
with one another
Oh knotted muscles
Oh the grid of muscles
who is playing from behind the body
who is singing boarded up in the body
meaning itself has been violated
by a horny copywriter
who brought about the plague of the crack
the plague of the hole
thus spake the hole

let there be a hole
the mango boys
in a chill-out trance
dance the hole
in the revelation lights of the Dome*

Hey you
in a blooming tree a bird sings
imagine it as yellow or black
or yellow black
it is there
unseen
for you haven't sought it

---

* A nightclub in Tel Aviv (footnote in the original).

Signal, Flicker

I sit in the dark
in a humming spring breeze
the sea simulating a parcel of land
nearly invisible
emitting a coldish stillness
no roar from its depths
the riptide has abated
and in its empty vastness
the cry subsided

And in the field of black water
a fisherman's sailboat
smallish because distant
glides in the slowest slowness
perhaps even stopping
flickering a yellow light
and so creating a parallel
offering itself as a simile
perhaps a simile to a simile

And yet gradually
I let go
of the sailboat analogy
and spread open to sea and sky
even blend in the darkness
that is new and refreshing
spotted with fresh stars
and a moon hangs in it
resembling a very large banana

Everything hints at something
everything signals and flickers
everything is itself and other
even the bicycle
leaning next to me against a bench
will demarcate a line between sea and home
will cross the air of the night
as stars drop on my head

What Will I Tell

And what will I tell myself?
That I am all right
that my story is compelling and appealing
even if its ending is clear and unclear at once?

I have spent my life writing poems
that are quite good
they have followers and buyers
fans critics translators and commentators
I've also contemplated several subjects
mostly relating to spirituality and spirit
and have published my contemplations
that are quite original and worthy
I've also treated quite a few people
who were acute complexities
who were wells of pain
their souls bearing open wounds
from real or imaginary battles
and I've loved
I've loved in a great fire
in the tumult of poems
and when at last I sobered up
from the wonderful hormone of illusion
I still had in me softness and kindness
a spirit of friendship and sincere concern
in short I'm a good guy
deserving of affection and even love
not to mention a measure of appreciation

But why am I telling you all this
who needs it
the judges in the other world
are still delaying the day of judgment
and what am I hiding from them
and from you
and from myself
in this carefully edited story
so very humble
so suspect, rousing suspicion

Poems About My Left Eye

1.

My left eye went dim
and turned into the evil eye
a disc of blood on the retina
caused an apocalyptic eclipse
but the right eye keeps winking consolation:
Soon you will be respectfully associated
with Homer Milton and Borges

The saw of fear sawing in my brain
subsides somewhat when the eternity
of poetry offers time
beyond time
a pause between closing the left eye
and closing the right eye
and even helps a bit to forget
the negligible repute of poetry
in a world of images and idols

But better than a poem is a blind cat
who survives in the streets among odors and sounds
and endows me with seven souls

2.

My blurry eye demands
a focused dogged gaze
to cross over to seeing
through the murky screen
but the clear eye
smug as ever
believes in her vision
even though she can only see
what she shows

The dim one sees the seer
but the clear one always forgets
who sees and who shows

3.

One eye sharp
and one eye dim
together they form a perfect vision
a perpetual parable
to the necessary flaw
of vision and observer
who is it who stands behind me
what is it that's fluttering above me
what is the void under me
and who is it who stands before me
know
before what
you
stand*

---

* Alludes to: "Know Before Whom You Stand," often inscribed above the ark in synagogues.

4.

On the bus
a chubby-nearly-fat girl
tries to peek into the notebook
I'm writing in
furtively seeking to connect
with the secrets of my soul
I shut the notebook
before her greedy eyes
and she sneezes heartily two or three times
as if scheming to connect
through a shared flu
as if airborne viruses
would join our souls

5.

The blindness spreading in my left eye
is the closing of the eye
toward a certain target
but where is the arrow
and what is the target
I once knew
where and what
but in the meantime I forgot
and a fog spreads
over the old perceptions

Am I now the target of the arrow
and who is pulling the bow
the angel of dots?

6.

The blindness spreading in my left eye
if it spreads to the right as well
an opaque curtain will stand
between me and the world
when I no longer can
tolerate the world
when I no longer can abide too much reality
my eyes retreat inwardly
concealing and contrasting
contemplating division and negation

7.

And this too from the left eye:
Don't examine death too closely
don't fix it with your stare
because in its fist
there's only blinding emptiness
never again will you be enchanted with the ficus tree foliage
with the flight of herons over rippling waters
with the glow of the moon and stars
reflected in the inky sea
and with the beauty of strangers

8.

Blessed are you king of the universe*
who endowed me with a hormone
that allows me to see you
more beautiful and wondrous than you are
that creates you precisely
according to the needs of my soul
I will bless you
even if the delusion of lust
that attracts the eye
that turns the eye into a hunter
is a sure formula for bitter regret

9.

Waiting in line for my eye exam
my pupil wide open
I read the poems of Pessoa—
"What have I done with life"—
a sort of defense against the colonel of fate
his poems empower me
in a moment of feeblemindedness
to believe that I had written them myself
as if I were his heteronym
or he my heteronym
his poems know my life
in such a great precise graceful way
that a spark of genius
glows on my forehead as well
as we chant together the hymns of Ecclesiastes

---

* From the prayer book, variation of: "Blessed art thou God our God king of the universe."

10. THE REALITY OF NEGATION

The lovers I never had
the spouse I never met
the kids I never raised
the books I never read
the parents I never had
the musings I never mused
the foot of lofty mountains
the cities I never visited
the cities not yet built
whose futuristic forms I haven't imagined
the identities I haven't realized
the indolence that makes you content with your life
as if others live for you
the greater part of life which you avoided
as well as the future that is not to flourish again

11.

I read the poems of Alvaro de Campos
by Pessoa
and I say to myself
this is the poet I was supposed to be
and he had been already
in all his unattainable fullness
well, it's okay—
I may hang out under a tree
and dream up a different destiny
colossally superficial
a fate in the burlesque style

12.

Distinguish between your eyes
let the right one be the rule of justice
and the left the rule of mercy
sharp eye—justice
dim eye—mercy
and the third eye for beauty—profound excruciating terrible
and the fourth eye—for the green winged beauty
and the fifth eye—for knives and needles and poisons
and the sixth eye—the center of the compass's needle
and the seventh eye for the invisible

Poems of the River

LEAVE BEHIND

Leave behind progress
go sit under a leafy tree
and observe the luminous water
listen to the birds sing
as they fly croon and never tire
all their tongues blend
intoning in choirs
trilling and fluttering
chirping and calling
some a green voice
some a black voice
and there's also lavender
mysterious songs
beyond your comprehension
and yet entirely apprehensible
in the deep brain, the ancient
the dormant

*

All at once
with no preparation or intent on my part
the ocean of infinity was revealed

The play of lights
on the dark water of the neighborhood river
the hum of distant roads
spilling into the empty lilac of the horizon
the jittery waves in the soft alien sea
into which the river flows—
all spoke of its presence

I did not ask to be lost in it
and I did not fear to exist in it
as a tiny speck

With lucid delight
I perceived the blind giant
in whose palm the planet spun
and I mulled over my mystifying ability
to overlook day after day
his immense presence

An Ecological Poem

In the green and generous moment
the greenery's green intensified
as the dense shrubbery of the river
was reflected quivering in the water
and the air was warm
holding a stillness
in which a chorus of birds trilled
and even the flutter of their wings was heard
and even the darting of the fish
was heard from a distance
while hum and rustle played in the warm hush

And at the same green and generous moment
my essence folded into the landscape
and I became a branch poised over water
I became a young and sparkling water turtle
and even a flock of green parakeets
and willingly donated my corpse
to the feast of worms insects and birds of prey
who rapaciously devoured its flesh
and I considered with serenity
the empty bench
that will wait here for another poet
if evolution will allow for poets

Rivers

Our dinghy sailed upon sweet waters
that flowed pure from a wondrous source
father paddled the oars
mother shuddered with the dinghy's jolts
and I lived in the certainty
of a boy who has parents
father and mother were my parents
I had origins
we sailed together in the dinghy
sail on sail on my dinghy*

Later I despaired and drowned
I became a water child
an orphan living in the depths of the river
with the other water kids
among intelligent and silent fish
amazing daffodils
transparent multi-legged crabs
and innumerable reflections
upside down worlds doubled and multiplied
a trap of a maze allowing no escape

---

* A children's song.

Slowly

Slowly slowly slowly
bring yourself over to slowness
and behold the core of the hidden
due to speed and acceleration

The shaded river
seems desolate and grim
the oily green glass of the water
empty
as the water birds
gather in the distance
where a kind Russian boy
scatters crumbs

But after I've given myself over
to foliage and greenery
to the flickering world of dark green
the gaping mouths of fish
surfaced for an instant
from the water and vanished
diving back
into their secret activities in the depths
leaving behind ripples
tiny and quiet green circles
that keep expanding evermore
until they're gone

And a beige eucalyptus leaf
slowly dropped
from a eucalyptus branch
leaning over the still green surface
and it contained all of death
if with great calm

And a white butterfly gracefully flew by
and offered the soul its form
embodying the miracle of life

and a flash

Word

Day after day
I retrace my steps
to come back and watch
what I have seen before
understand anew the understood
actually no
actually to see
to know in seeing
to know in touching
to know in listening
in sheer being
to know being
here are the grasses
here are damp green stones
                                in the murky river
a blackbird and a crow
and invisible others
hidden in foliage and light
chirping and singing and cawing
and a sudden fishing bird
soaring and gliding
swiftly plunging into small fishes
outlining a word in the air
in hieroglyphics
spelling bird

Green

All is green
grass blades green
the trembling eucalyptus foliage green
the screaming parrots in the foliage green
the flat murky river green
and in every green a multitude of greens
multiplying in water mirrors
in damp and shiny emeralds
and as my eyes observe all this green
I touch a great joy
that devotedly has been waiting for me
all through summer

*

I've forgotten my aging
and the field dreaming my corpse
and I became a bird of the river
in one dive
I snared a small silvery flapping fish
and speedily eluded the seagulls
that sought to seize my catch

And I vanished in the blue

Buddies

On the hill shaded by ficus and pine trees
a girl and four boys
before my astonished eyes
one fondles her breasts
another strokes her thighs
and she flutters as if objecting
and a third, as if in jest, knocks back her attackers
and they all finally sit on the bench
her curly head resting on the thigh
very near the crotch
of the boy who squeezed her breasts

A handsome redhead boy
well-toned and taller than his friends
perhaps older than they
not sitting not intervening
he keeps a measured distance
reading a sheet of paper

I intervene:
"What would your mother say if she saw you now"
and at once lasciviousness dissolves
all become mother's good boys
the chorus of birds coos and trills
crows pigeons blackbirds

Their classmates arrive on the hill
with a young teacher in a floral dress
with great rumpus the seventh graders take a pop-quiz
Who was Dizengoff, Who was Usishkin,
the questions are answered and they all depart
the friends also leave the hill
riding their colorful bikes
and the song of birds is heard again
crows pigeons blackbirds

Only the handsome boy is left
slowly rearranging his backpack
oblivious to the calls of his friends
he takes his time with his bike
and nearly rides away without his helmet
having left it forgotten on the bench
I call after him
and he returns and slowly puts it on
a gleaming red helmet on his red head
with care he pulls on his logoed gloves
and mounts his bike again
quickly circling round toward me
and descends the hill taking a different path
longer from the one his friends have chosen

Even after he disappeared
in the humming shade alive with birds
his figure still lingered on the hill
asking to be burnt in my gaze
and it was burnt and written

A Short Story

A skinny baby heron
tottered frightened near the bushes
seeking to hide
from its predators
I went past it
with the speed of my bike
and noted to myself: cute
a cute anxious heron
about an hour later
again on my bike
the heron already lay
encircled by crows
a red hole in its white belly

A blow to the heart
I loathed its killers
that banded together to butcher it
black assassins
of a white gosling, a tender soul
and yet the preying crows
love the heron
as do the ants
and also the worms
and the sand as well
all are hungry and in love
with their young meal—a baby heron
they all feed on with love
never with hate

Just imagine
no love no hate
no sorrow no mercy
not in the devourer and not in the devoured
only need
profit and loss
simple economics
and this morning I am the weak one
the gosling, the sacrificial, the paranoid
thirsty for love
rustling like bulrush

Water

Narcissus did not fall in love with his image
but with water
for its divine mysterious ability to reflect his image
and the overhanging tree branches
and the ever changing skies
and the herds of drifting clouds
water has endowed those reflected
with magnificent doubles glowing as if anointed
with holy moments of eternity
until dusk came and then darkness

The charms of water so enthralled him
that he preferred the reflections over the reflected
every day he swam in the sky
among clouds among tree branches
his soul seeking to be like water
and like it to contain the entire cosmos
and become the form of many

His studies of reflections
initiated investigations that others pursued
even after he turned
into a flower a frog and a worm
perhaps even a tear or a puddle

From the investigations rose the foundations of our culture:
the looking-glass, painting, and the camera

*

The bird dives
and catches a fish
the fish flutters in its beak
perhaps dancing
in the blue of the sky
the rock 'n roll of death
a moment before the digestive tract
of a fairly small bird
quite delicate in fact
and God will consume them both

Only a Moment

In the grove near the river
the breeze is warm and gentle
and everywhere the choirs of birds
cooing and chirping
in the fan-like spread of shadows and leaves
crowing amid leftovers

On the paving stones burnt charcoals
a Hover Disc cigarette butts empty cans golden candy wrappers
a cherry chewing-gum wrapper
and here comes a beautiful Ethiopian boy
slender and graceful as a deer
a gold earring in his earlobe
employed by City Hall
to pick up litter with a stick—
Ethiopian?
Yes
How old?
Nineteen

He kept it short and quickly left
briskly stabbing refuse
down the grassy lawns
not at all tempted
to have a fling with a bicyclist
                                        of a certain age

I too want to leave
but I am stuck to the bench with gum
already alluded to before
and as I scrub the seat of my pants
the gum spreads its cherry scent
and the birds all around look like
black holes in the air
flying holes
scarier than Hitchcock's birds

I've placed a leaf on the gooey cherry-gum
to spare others
the trap of the bench
and flew away from there on my bike
hungry the hunger of lunch

I Wanted to Tell You

I wanted to tell you something
but now I no longer know
if I'll ever be able to say it
I even worry
that without noticing
I may have already said
what I wanted to say
that during one crucial moment
quite ordinary
and mysterious as a sealed shell
the future had already become past
and I wonder if
when I spoke to you
articulating the thing
if you actually heard
if you listened
for I myself did not listen
having no idea I'd finally spoken

And if I have yet to say what needs to be said
will it become clear in the future
what is the correct true word
will you then listen to it
in other words listen to me
will you accept what's coming?
Meantime at any rate
bye-bye and so long

from *Tamir's Poems* (2007)

Tamir's Poems—a book-length cycle of love poems. The title—crediting Tamir as the creator of the poems—and the love poems are very much in the spirit of the twelfth-century Sufi mystic Rumi. Rumi's love poems for Shams, *The Works of Shams of Tabriz,* inspired Geldman, who wrote most of *Tamir's Poems* in Anatolia, Turkey, not far from Konya, where Rumi is buried, and where he attributed his love poems to Shams.

Inscribed

Now comes the hour of the setting sun
now comes the time to revel in it
the sun will turn and set*
and I will love you with all my might†
and you will love me as you can
until light gathers into the bosom of darkness

And when night prevails you will handle my corpse
take me to a lovely plot
erect a stone and inscribe it
"Here rests a happy man
who in the lengthening twilight
when all the shades of red ignite
he loved was loved and he sang"

---

* Alludes to the Ne'ila service on Yom Kippur.

† Alludes to "And thou shalt love the Lord thy God with all thine heart, and with all thy soul, and with all thy might." (Deut. 6:5).

Let Me

Let me kiss you on the mouth
*I would prefer not to**
Let me embrace your slender body
I would prefer not to
Let me suck you a little
I would prefer not to
Let me fuck you good
I would prefer not to
And if you wish I'll be your bottom
I would prefer not to

Then what do we need this togetherness for
and how will it all end for us?

What's so bad though?
I'm the desired in your desire
I'm the wanted boy
you the old the rebuffed
you are the spurned
in whom the aphrodisiac of rejection
stirs up youthful hormones
and poems
and please know as well
that you are the best of my friends
and I love you
love you very much
in my own way

---

* English in the original, alludes to Melville's Bartleby.

Similes

You give of yourself only partially
refusing to give me your body
yet my body doesn't give up, it persists

Am I not like Ahab
chasing across the vast ocean
after a white whale
a primordial creature of the depths
whose formidable motion
may yet break my boat
sink it under the breakers

Still, I'd rather stick to the eastern mentality
to depict my state of utter sentimentality
I've become addicted to chasing after deer
I'm the hunter with an arrow in his heart
I'm the hunted hunter
hunted by the deer

True Compassion

You probably won't believe this
but when my love for you first flared up
I considered above all how you would handle my corpse
when my time came
I thought that I had found at last
and just in time
a forthright and gentle soul
who would do right managing my burial
who would show me true compassion
if I died all alone
and in my fancy I repay you well in advance
offer you all my assets
all of my being
I empty all of myself unto you
so that I may remain
so that I may remain in you
like a father remains in his son

Gift

The birthday gift you bought for me
bespeaks the unspoken:
an object of fine glass
inlaid with white lace
a round candle receptacle
intimating that you will guard my soul
in your delicate fragile soul
and that you hope
I will shelter the candle of your soul
in the luminosity of my soul
and these three notebooks
are to contain the words of my soul
the poems of my soul
the poems of our love
which I've already begun composing in secret

And as to the body—yours, mine, ours,
you say, Let's leave it for now,
at least for the moment

60

In two days I'll turn sixty
and you are thirty-two
only thirty-two

How can I hope for you to desire my body
when you favor youngsters like yourself
and ever younger strapping youths?
Still, passions roil in me
I'm awash in powerful hormones
from a source I thought had dried up
and this without holding in my consciousness
a clear vision of your body
or an image of sexual intimacy

It seems that my lust longs to embrace your soul
that hormones are not what stirred my love
but the other way around
my love for your essence stirred my body

I'm sixty
but I lust like an adolescent
and this very same adolescent muddles the aged
even makes him dumb

Cell Phone

When I purchased a new cell phone
I soon realized my mistake
I should have got one identical to yours
since I'm in love with yours
in love with its silly cheery ringtone
from your cell come text messages
I await with a longing heart
through your cell phone the din of my brooding and babbling
pours into your ear
and your pals too call the cell
all the guys and youngsters
from the bars, the gyms, the parties,
a sect I was expelled from decisively
due to my looming birthday
and among the callers there is one
you will surely sleep with
tonight or tomorrow
and this bitter knowledge
sets my love on fire

The Spirit and the Soul

Hey Tamiri sweetie
I hereby offer you my Buddhist head
balding and ever-smiling
severed from my neck with my own hands
offered to you like Yochanan's* was offered to Salomé

Now I am a wholly illumined being:
the final and absolute truth is eh . . .death†
after which truth is named

The spirit knows this
and seeks to deaden my desire
so that I may reach my hour
as a dead who could die no more
or be reborn into a karmic cycle
one who can no longer hold onto the lily
onto your gentle murmurings
onto the evening movements of clouds
onto the vision of a field after dawn

And yet the enamored soul
tossed between pain and pleasure
clinging to the everyday and the transient

---

* John the Baptist.

† In the Hebrew: "eh . . .met" combine to Emet—Truth—while "met" alone means dead.

and even to death which it abhors
invites us both to a dance
in which will flash the three subtleties
of your cyclamen charm
a gift you will grant no one but me
for only I can perceive it

Worry

I do worry
that it is me who I love in you
that the cyclamen vulnerability in you
which so captivated my compassion
and so stirred my passion for you
is in fact my own vulnerability

For it is possible that my work
is just to compensate for a bitter judgment
I could not overrule
by which an imposed paucity prescribed my days
to make me alien alone and solitary
drifting toward emptiness
wherever I turn

I am like you: a slave of need

And now I have become Everyman
whom time disgraces and desiccates
like a cyclamen in the pages of a book

I Dreamt You

I dreamt you long ago:
I was working in a remote nursery
moving dirt from one planter to another
when I spotted among the clay pots
one in which a field had sprouted
a field of tiny violet cyclamen
taking my breath away

I pointed out the field
to everyone present
but no one could see it
so tiny was the vast field

For the field was mine alone
the field of my vision
of my cyclamen
of you as only I can see you

Another Bracelet

Next morning I went back to the store
and requested a bracelet for myself
a twin to yours
which together will form a pair of handcuffs
or a new brand of wedding bands
but my heart disallowed the purchase
a stubborn defiance choked my throat

I left the store perturbed yet determined
but soon reconsidered
telling myself
I should gift you two bracelets rather than one
so when you find your chosen one
you'll give him a bracelet as a wedding handcuff
tears came to my eyes
as I sought to bravely allow
that sooner or later
you'll marry a beautiful youth
whom I'll desire too
in my heart of hearts

You are mine I am yours
I did not purchase the bracelet
not for me, not for you

Deer

You illumine for me
an image Arab poets
chose for the boy of their lust—
the deer

The deer grazes grass off your hand
its tongue delicately dampens your palm
but an abrupt move
a sudden leaf rustle
will send him leaping at once
to graze elsewhere

I am therefore cautious
forever fearful you'd be frightened and flee
or that if hurt you'd willfully turn inward
claim that you never loved me
that your soul never sought mine
and that your declarations of love ("non-romantic")
were just a momentary whim
and that you still lust
after any passing stranger

The Date

And after my lust for you had ignited
we set a date in your apartment
and I brought along a blooming plant
and hastened to tell you my thoughts
all about the roads open before us
and I asked you to touch my face
which you did
and I too touched your face
and then I asked that you kiss my face
leaving no facial spot unkissed
which you did
and I too kissed you
yet you refused to cross over to fondling
but in the interim
my soul had been struck
gripped by light and pain
as dormant depths revived

The Son

Angels did not foretell his arrival
but just before the closing of the gates
very near my sixtieth birthday
when despair had already erased all hope
I found a son in you
if indeed you'd be willing

I, the barren, the solitary, the forlorn,
found succor and relief
in your desire to be a son
in your quest for a loving father
you never had

And you won't be my son forever
you'll end up a father to me
you'll find me a strong and handsome Filipino
who will diaper me with a sure hand
who will take me for walks in the neighborhood
or will push my wheelchair
to the lovely riverbank
his arm my support

Eurydice

During the eight years of friendship
preceding the rush of my love
I kept telling you
that because of your passive demeanor
you seemed to me
like a piece of driftwood
floating aimlessly downstream

Yet now I imagine you as Eurydice
who naturally dies
while Orpheus sings and plays in the Underworld
to bring her back to the land of the living

See how many poems I've written
to bring you back to life
to awaken and stir your soul
I, whose death is near and evident,
call out to you to come to life
move, go out, seize, hold onto something
plot your story

Please, do not anger over my blunt words
they are truer than the mundane vacuous
chatter of your suitors

Rumi

Leisurely, I walked down the street
looking up at the mountains
the snowy peaks visible in the distance
it was hot even though spring had just begun

And when I stopped for tea
Jalal ad-Din Rumi turned up in my mind
Rumi, whose love for Shams, his pupil, the young blacksmith,
stirred great poems in his soul
and I marveled at the process repeating
in the mind of a Tel Aviv poet
not far from the grave
in Konya

I kissed his cheeks
my lips grazed his perfumed beard
I held his hand
and led him out to the street
to walk arm in arm as is the Turkish custom
and on the way, Tamir, we encountered you
and you gave us a reticent look

For what is to you the intoxication
with the beautiful and the sublime
or the joy in a celestial companion
you who hunt for joy in gyms

I'm harsh with you, Tamir,
my words are brutal,
yet I keep in mind that you share
in all my poems

There's Love

They say there's love
but where is it—in me, in you, in us both?
My love flows from my heart
independent of my lover's favors
my love rushes outward, to the open,
like an arrow from the bow
I am my beloved's even if my beloved isn't mine*
as he consorts with others
and yet has stamped me with love

My love is a banner
as well as a sermon addressed
to all fornicators in saunas, backyards, clubs
                                        latrines, gyms,
to all who cling to the slick body-wall
to all who are blind to the soul and deny it
to all who copulate body to body
and stubbornly refuse
                    to know one another
as if foreskin has sealed their hearts
and a hazy lust of the senses
rules the bodies that worship bodies
those enslaved to the cock to the toned muscle the smooth skin
the naked scented shadows in dark rooms
those lost in glory holes and golden showers
those deviating to the pole of pleasure

---

* Alludes to and alters Song of Songs 6:3: "I am my beloved's, and my beloved is mine."

Please look to the soul
to the opal agate and amethyst*
chase after love
stir and arouse the heart
seek the soul in its mysteries
aim to attain the gifts of the spirit

Take a look Tamir
our love is both proof and reproof
to those body worshippers of the barren soul

* Alludes to Exodus 28:16, detailing the precious stones in the outer garment of the High Priest in the Temple.

And Now

And now what will become of us
now that my poems granted our passion
a vastness bordering the infinite
how will we withstand the quotidian
how will we carry on with our everyday forms?
For have you not taken fright at the tumult of my feelings
at the revelation of my soul's wings
at the visions that revealed your own soul
in images you never even imagined?
And will you accept your new eminence
as the master of transformation and inspiration
or that of the silent siren?
And what will become of us
now that I've turned your refusal
into the driving force of a strange triumph
that may seem insignificant to you?

But it is possible
that as I have submitted myself to your inspiration
your heart with my inspiration will open
to transform your deferred refused life
and a tide of emotion will dissolve the frozen in you
until at last you reach the source
from where my essence flows
and your will too will flow there
granting you a charm that will never fade

As for me, for the time being
I'm reeling like a dervish
and already I've envisioned the great tree
blooming in the spring of the self
in lilac splendor
blissful and inebriated

Text Messaging Poems

1.

Because you seduced me and then refused me
my soul spread its wings
to seduce you with its beauty
but it only scared you away

2.

Because your spirit is still incomplete
I felt I had to complement you
add onto you from my soul
fill in all that was missing
and you became my perfect lover

3.

In the blinding mountain light
where we walked yesterday
each of us speculated about the other
yet what we observed was somewhat incomplete
there are things we were afraid to see

4.

In the still vastness of the mountains
we are one and another
but two as well

5.

The blue thistle of our love
sprouts from the reluctant and the aching
I am not the boy you wish for
your double your striking figure
and because of your blindness
you'll probably never know me

6.

"If I gave you all my love
no love would remain in the world"

7.

I was horny for you
but I screwed Uriel
the tattooed biker with the angel face
in my imagination you became one

8.

At times because of your reluctance
I roused your jealousy
but when you ignited mine
you wished to hurt me
to subdue me even more

9.

Without a hint of guilt
you were pleased to discover
you possessed a caustic charm
and clever seduction ploys
my pain was a gift

10.

Passion invents its object
as lust subsides
only you remain
namely less

11.

A rare and vicious narcissus
made believe it was a delicate cyclamen
or perhaps you are both
narcissus and cyclamen

12.

Lamb and wolf wolf and lamb
your wolf devoured the lamb
in you in me
and so we remained two wolves
malice lodging in our hearts

13.

Measured against my ideal mate
you're but a blurred sketch
worse—a negative

14.

If I hadn't persisted in
saving you from yourself
if my soul hadn't pursued its destroyer
to be born again
before its time came
you couldn't have hurt me

15.

There's a cold place in your brain
a place of pure selfishness
the source of your malice
a place created by fear
secret but formative
that you're not worthy
of love or even passion
this place is our divide
always and forever

16.

You're like Borat's sister
exposing her cunt
before her slow brother
whispering
you won't get it you won't get it

17.

As you've roused my feminine side as well
I also felt like becoming a bottom
a delicious emasculation
that would have been even sweeter
had you said yes

18.

All my love
all my lust
were gifts from the Jew the Christian
and the Buddhist in my heart
granted me to heal what you lack
but I also imagined a cock and a hole
natural—no?

19.

To whom have I sent my messages
to an inner being my fancy depicted
to a cyclamen a wolf another entity?
And who's the one who replies
who's the one who delays his response
who's the one who doesn't reply
who are you
will I ever be able to see you?

20.

Not this not that
not a cyclamen not a narcissus
not a wolf not a lamb
aim for the empty spot
from which you will grow
from which the right person will emerge
one who knows the other with warmth
whose assets are love and a vessel

21.

The bond between us cannot last
if your lust drives you to others
I gave you up for all of them
the guys from the gyms the bars
the clubs and so on.
Goodbye.

22.

The cruel temptation brought about my poems.
If foreplay had fulfilled its promise
if my lust had been satisfied
you wouldn't have been the heart of my inspiration
we wouldn't have had poems and text messages
in the malice there had been a grace that kindled grace
granted to us both
with amazing generosity

Sixty

When I turned sixty
I saw in my face a naked skull
reflected in the mirror
and I became a frightened man
but against the gaping void
your slender dark silhouette suddenly appeared
stirring in me such a powerful passion
I could no longer see the point
of reading the paper building towers traveling to distant lands
wishing for glory making wars hoarding wealth
making philosophy
when the essential truly is being with you
chatting or listening to music or going for a walk
with you
you who so resemble the boys
I made out with in my youth
in the backyards of South Tel Aviv
with you
who had ignited in me the lust of the rejected
because you favored embracing and soulful conversations
denying me the naked the sexual a hole

Clearly it was a delusion
a mirage
granted me by an enchanting and merciful goddess
through her son the handsome archer
a delusion that means
becoming a servant of Eros
who in his gardens of tangled bushes

conceals from view the river of death and oblivion
that sooner or later will sweep me away
a delusion that means I'd better convert
and worship like you in fitness temples
worship innocent youths
their tattooed muscles
and so hide from my death in your being
in the being of an eternal boy
standing with open arms under a cascading waterfall
maturity as inaccessible to him
as hieroglyphics
and making out with boys
the essence of his life

A generous goddess granted me this
but something impenetrable in your nature—
a strange and alien charm
a psychopathic Eros a cruel temptation
entrapped my consciousness in your illusion
or perhaps I was driven by rejection and deferral
perhaps you've become the essential
against which all else is trivial
because of what you denied me
you became the denied love
the love denied me beforehand as ever
from the moment of my birth
and I with a queer tenacity
set out on a last battle to conquer it
in your boyish immature heart

How could I, Tamir

How could I, Tamir,
not to succumb
to the roguish enticements that roused my passion
to your ploys designed to rouse both my jealousy and my lust?
In a curve in the desert
one nomad came upon another
but our bond has lent gravity
to Time
for between our dates I waited for our dates
when I rose in the morning I knew why
and nights when I lay in my bed
it is you I thought of
                                until I drowned in dreams
I nearly forgot who I was and who I was not
what I've accomplished and what I have not
what I was lacking and lacking more and more
most of my faces vanished
and with them the skull of the dead
I became one man united in longing
and my passion rose powerful and turbulent
like the passion of wild boys
it never diminished and never will
it became timeless like a force of nature
in my delusion I discovered the absolute

How could I, Tamir,
not to succumb to your schemes
even as my Jewish Christian Buddhist heart
knew you had nothing to offer
except seduction
except that corrupted cyclamen corona
of the eternal boy always in pursuit of his lusts?
Could I have prevented you
from abducting me
from ruling me
from becoming the lording master of my heart?
But if not for your cunning seduction
your void would have opened before us
a void greater and more dreadful than my own
a void that could never be filled
the void of the foretold loser
the void of the denier and the hater
and my love all of my love
a love greater than I'd ever known
would have been necessary for us
to make you and I forget
that behind the attractive figure where you've taken refuge
no other self is hidden
and certainly not an enlightened self
be it only in the ashen light of dawn
and yet I hope that my love for you
will erect in your heart a small temple
wherein the cycle of poems I wrote
will become like a vessel overflowing with love
from which you will drink and drink more
when the cruel thirst awakens in you
when the cruelest thirst
the most basic need
stirs in you
until you finally rise toward your hidden self
your taciturn form

Is it possible that my passionate love for you
essentially sprang from your future form?

After we parted
in my dream I gave you four gifts
three of them I couldn't recognize
and the fourth, a keepsake locket:
two squares of pure gold
enclosing our picture
face to face
and between us a dark circle
like a dot or a hole—
I lay my gift before you

from

Poem of the Heart

(2004)

Home Poems

1.

I am the only son of nomads
whom a cruel god they had created
kept banishing from their homes time after time
sending them to wander in deserts

I am the son of nomads
whose last homes
were burnt by homicidal platoons, officers of death
who decreed new lodgings for them:
convict huts, mass graves, heaps of ashes, chimneys,
tunnels, cellars, gutters, the thick of forests

And in the holy parched land
on the shore of a sparkling blue sea
our new home erupted time and again
ablaze in the heat of quarrels
vanquished in memories and phantoms
slayers bursting out of my father's body
an imaginary pistol his weapon
victims emerging from my mother's heart
who became a serial suicide
and our home whirled like a vortex upon its void

2.

I built my first home in a massive ficus tree
birds were my mother and father
chicks were my brothers
an ant became my cousin
and in my ficus home I hid my belongings
a minuscule notebook
a crayon of twilight colors
theater glasses
and a few booklets
about a naked white man in the jungle
and I had a cache of leaves
untouched by fall
where I sought to be an immortal child of no memories
a child of the present
whose god is a pansy
and his faith a ficus
but on the distant arid mountains
there stood the house of a terrible god
a burnt offering smoldering on its altar

3.

In brown cardboard boxes
I hid as if inside a home
their velvety darkness my blanket
at times I took shelter in a closet
dreaming the life of a wandering clochard
sleeping under bridges
our backyard too
was a refuge and hiding place
there a boy kissed a boy on his cheek and mouth
and the sand became a primordial valley
where magic stones whirred
monsters shrank to insect-size
and treasures—
all gifts of the sand

Who was the one who was hiding
and what was he hiding from
after all the god whose one eye is foul
and his other eye pure
nothing is hidden from him

At First I Wished to Speak Up

At first I wished to speak up
and didn't know how and what
a commotion stirred in my heart
yet I didn't know what it was and why
and when at times I did speak
I hid more than I revealed
I spoke and spoke yet the core remained unspoken

But now that my speech is fluent
I no longer need you to listen
no longer seek to speak or formulate
I seek my comfort in silence
pass over your blindness
like an inmate fleeing the prison of words
I'll hide in a cave of stillness
will suckle silence from wisdom's teat
and will suspend my words from interim to interim
and will listen—will listen with all my might
and every morn I'll mold on a potter's wheel
a black jug to contain my secret

Form

All he ever wanted was a form—
at times it was revealed to him in boys
at times in paintings
in old ruins or poems
and at times even in frogs or birds
in other words a living breathing form
even if by its nature it meant a shrinking
that evokes the eternal
like a black-flaming panther or an urn
or an acrobat flying through air

He sought after his form
like one fleeing formlessness
he sought after his form
with great desperation
he sought after a form
that would be admired by all
because his parents his progenitors
had willed his excellent form
because the form of his parents
had been broken by polished officers of murder
who murdered even their own god

And yet his father and mother
who ardently willed his excellent form
continuously gnawed at his form
always hungering after it

and so his form became consumed and beset
and his hunger for a complete form was never sated or relieved
and his form became his way and custom
and seeking after his form became his form
and his form became his god

But when his god obliged him
and his form took on light and song
he felt himself trapped in the narrow and confined
and he turned to other gods
that have no form or face
the god of want
whose absence is the origin of forms
whose absence is the origin of all want of all that's wanting
a god of chaos and confusion
an infinite emptiness
and from the emptiness he sought to wrest his form
and he cast his net in the void

The Neurotic's Poem

If only I had more money
If only I had sex at least once a day
If only I met the right man
If only I had a fling with a Butoh dancer
If only I were better understood
If only I could fit in a Zen convent
If only I could live near Ravello
If only I had neighbors who are not survivors of the camps
If only my neighbor, the delicate Miss Universe, preferred me to her
    Chihuahua
If only I were a prose writer rather than a poet
If only I were much younger
If only I came across the right books
If only I had one good teacher
If only you could love me as much as I love you
If only I had saner parents
If only I'd known the truth at the opportune time
If only I were better equipped for happiness
If only I were a better liar
If only I were less faithful to myself
If only I were an optometrist or a veterinary for chimpanzees
If only I'd begun doing yoga sooner

If only I were in my being and not in my want

*

The voice of a bird woke me from my afternoon nap
whether it was the voice of a pelican
or the voice of a water bird
pausing on the bushes in the yard
I didn't know
but yearning and want sounded in its voice
the vastness of evil skies
and a gloomy complaint

Nature is hungry, I mused.
Is the Buddha sated
when satiety itself is a hunger for hunger?

Poet

When she died
many came to the funeral
those who when she lived shaped the vastness of her loneliness
as if they had gathered there to thank her
for dying
a self-made death
removing from their world
her provocative demanding tragic presence
leaving behind her
what is easy to take
and even allows exultation
a collection of sparkling poems
that adorned Hebrew with splendid crowns
even though they spoke of great longing
even her longing for death

Oh My Love

For Amit, the motorcycle stuntman, killed in an accident in 2009

Oh how much I love you
crazy for you crazy for you
the pain of love cruises eel-like
in all my blood vessels
when I bring you into my rooms
when I greedily drink in your saliva
or suck you
or lick you from head to toe
overlooking nothing
and my thorough licking nearly finishes you

Oh how much I love you
I'd dwell in your body for hours, entire nights
steadily moving in the rhythm of yearning
in the deep gate yielding to its pleasure
penetrating deeper and deeper toward the impenetrable
cooing the nonsense of pigeons
scheming to make you addicted to pleasure
and I would have allowed you to linger in my body
if you'd really wanted to

Yet as much as I love you
I discover my remoteness from your soul
for in fact I don't know you
and our acquaintance is not enough to know you
even if it lasted months and years
because you yourself are an enigma to yourself a hidden secret
and especially I dread the barrier of your body

And in fact the one who loves you
he too is not entirely known to me
and he too hides
in his body or in the mist of words

But listen to me my love
it is possible that my love for you
is only intended to transform you
into a person I know
a person I know as my lover
as someone who is first of all and after all
my lover
and being my lover is his essence
so I too will become clear and bewitched
our love my main attribute

Oh my love reveal your name
Oh my love speak my name

Love Poem

Access into our street was blocked—
an ambulance a flashing cruiser a fire truck
and overwrought residents
stood in my way home
foiling my desire to sprawl
in front of the TV screen
that offers the soul edited disasters

Our street is small and action-poor
no object was ever found suspect
no break-ins no screams
except for the wailing of cats in heat
or the cries of crows over the carcass of a cub
the gardens in our street are tidy
and the houses stand revamped in orderly rows
most of the residents are new and strong
youths perfumed with fresh perfumes
have taken the place of the old
the replacement of the aged by the young
is a hushed furtive process
an ambulance came and went
and hop—the elderly is gone
the funerary notices are discreet
the Filipino went back to the Philippines or found another elderly
but here suddenly an ambulance a cruiser and a fire truck
signaling together some horrific event
a tragedy for the daily paper:
at nine o'clock in the evening
when the street's skies are purple and hollow

a murder and a suicide
human blood
a man shot a woman and then himself
all because of unrequited love
all because of a woman's rejection
all because a mind rose up against itself
a final gesture to annul gesture

Even a retiring street like ours
cannot forestall the senses from going mad
cannot temper the fervor of love
even a small street poses a big question:
How much love is there in love?
"He took her, mamy"*
someone shouted into a cell phone
oy mamy
oy mamy

---

* Slang. A form of endearment, usually among Sephardic Jews.

N.B.

A second murder in a month
Mr. Nissim Bashi
whose initials connote
an afterthought in a letter*
was found dead in our neighborhood
in a parking lot in a small side street

N.B. was a tall man, handsome and dark-skinned,
whose gaze was both dull and febrile
like the gaze of a stealthy pervert
and whose secret dealings were known to all:
trading dollars and loans
the savior of the tax evader and the insolvent
and he would have gone on until a ripe old age
were it not for the Arab owner of the Laundromat
who chose to eliminate the creditor
rather than settle his debt

N.B. was found dead and bound in a four-wheeler
(a baby carriage or a supermarket cart)
as the murderer folded his murdered
like a parcel of ironed laundry
but the stain made by his knife
no wash will wash away
go figure—
a man spends his days removing our stains
as preparation for a stain that will never be removed

---

* n.b. is the Hebrew for p.s.

Go figure
the Arab in this Jewish story
who unwittingly incriminated himself
will continue his plot in prison
where he is fated to become a laundress
when he is forced by Jewish offenders
to take it from the rear

All at once our neighborhood
known as clean and quiet
has become violent and fraught with danger
for, it turns out, a killer or a victim
hides in every home
and I myself—a future killer, a future victim, or both—
am a man whose talent for tragedy is only partially realized

And what about my neighbor Esther
who day in and day out wished her husband
with shrieks heard by all the neighbors
"May you die already"?
Since his death she cries every day all day
Jacob Jacob
as if he were hiding behind a curtain
at home and not in Holon*

---

* A cemetery near Tel Aviv.

The Café

Like Stevens the smart poet
I too am certain that God
wishes things to be as they are

Bare-muscled hunks
sipping coffee
from white mugs
wherein spoons tinkle
stirring horny whipped cream
or let them sip mint soda
amidst vases bursting with flowers

He does not wish that all drop to their knees
to worship His temple in the east

God wishes
the moment to be filled with the momentary
and not only with His presence—
Praised and Blessed Be He The Emperor of Ice Cream

from

Oh My Dear Wall

(2000)

Poems of Mourning

*

In the depths of childhood
in a beginning as blind as matter
her body for me was a divine object
her soft breast, intoxicating,
was mine, mine alone, mine, mine

At the heart of the sea of reality
where countless menacing waves rose
her body for me was an island of softness
her soft breast, glowing, was mine, mine,
and she whispered in my ear, Mordechai lives
Mordechai lives

But now her body is being consumed
while her life tenaciously persists in her
since much suffering has been decreed for her
In a dream I saw all her suffering
I saw the suffering still hidden from her
and in the dream I wept

From childhood's grace she became future's edict
from childhood's mystery she became a terrible meaning
I plead for her
let her soul move on toward death

*

In the end I could not save her

I who had been appointed by her to save her
I who had saved her again and again since childhood
from the death that hummed in her
from the Poles the Germans from the neighbors from Father
and even from myself—
in the end I could not save her
all my efforts fell short
for in the end her time had come

In the end she knew nothing
except her death
that surged from within her like a conquering killer
and she, as if yearning for him without alarm,
placed herself in his hands

In the end she could only say—
"Shabbat is here"
as if all of time had been lost
and only Shabbat remained
a white dress she wore for her Shabbat
and all the days all day
she lit more and more Shabbat candles
and a Shabbat fire she lit on the stove
and perpetual light she lit in the bulbs*
and set the table for the Shabbat meal
as if waiting for me

---

* Alludes to Exodus 27:21: "And thou shalt command the children of Israel, that they bring thee pure oil olive beaten for the light, to cause the lamp to burn always."

as if waiting for Him
lecha dodi likrat kallah*

In the end the candles dimmed
and the white dress perished as well
for it was stained with food urine and excrement
and I who had been appointed to be her grace and glory
could not in the end save her
for all my efforts fell short

---

* From the liturgy, a song recited in synagogue Friday evening to welcome the Shabbat, referred to as a bride and queen: "Come my beloved to greet the bride." The beloved is often equated with God.

*

Before she died her soul died
her mind diminished and became muddled
even her name she forgot
and she stopped being a mother
and became every person
and I too was integrated in her
and we were all a burnt offering
and a great negation consumed the earth

But a little after she'd been interred in the soil
she returned and reunited with her name and character—
Eva-Hava Esther-Ishtar
she was my mother again
my forever lost mother
my ever lost mother

And all the mothers that raised me
from my beginning till my maturity—
the gentle and the kind
the wounded and the monstrous
they were all in her as one

And then others were suddenly included in her
many other women known and unknown
among them hidden women winged and luminous
and then silence and darkness and lamentation shrouded my soul

With my birth she was reborn
and with her death I died as well
for hours days a season
and with her death I too was redeemed
for I'd been saved from the torments of her life and her great misfortune

Firing Squad

The day of my mother's death arrived and then the hour came. She had to wait ten minutes for the firing squad to assemble but she remained calm. Her approaching death did not intensify her sorrow and her alarm was not roused. What is sorrow and what is alarm if she's been dead for a while and now in my dream they wish to kill her with a new death and a different method.

Chu

A monk asked Chao-Chu:
Is the nature of Buddha in the dog?
Ehhhh, said Chao-Chu

1.

A car ran over the cat Chu
and I wept for my cat Chu
(affectionately I called him Chu-Chu)
as if he were my son or my friend-beloved

But my weeping distressed me—
how can you, I said, cry for a cat
while death consumes people in its thousand mouths
the land is filled with widows and orphans
and many parents lost their sons
and he who didn't die in the war died in a terrorist attack
and he who didn't die in a terrorist attack
died in a car crash, floods, fires

And he who didn't die in those died from old age or illness
and he who didn't vanish in death
is now blind and lame or scarred with burns
and all are awaiting the next war
that will destroy even the birds and cats

2.

The cat Chu like most of the cats in our land
was a fourth-world citizen
living at the bottom of society's ladder
below the beer guzzling foreign workers
below the shaking drug-addicted whores
together with the litter-nibbling hobos

But I raised him from the gutter
to be a domestic noble tiger
a green-eyed striped tiger
daintily stepping on pillows and armchairs
feeding on Italian preserves
and choosing to catnap with his head in my palm

Am I an orphic poet who seeks
his beloveds in the lower worlds
who favors a stone the builders refused*
who imports his poems from the lands of death?

3.

At night Chu came to me in his spirit
and said in the language of humans:
"Now that you've written two poems
you're ready to forget me
but I'm a cat of three poems
if not more"

---

* From Psalms 118:22: "The stone which the builders refused is become the head stone of the corner."

The Wall

Fate's design was cruel
beyond the wall near my bed
fate installed new tenants: a young couple
a couple fitting a reality show
making love with moans and groans
and on other nights sweet nothings
and giggling till sleep comes

I who had trained in asceticism
I who for years had been accustomed
to the sleep of the solitary
am suddenly condemned to this peculiar torment
my bed now connected to their love-bed
as if I dwelled within their love
within their enticing whispers
within their young odors
in the rising clamor of their lust

How pretty the girl's chirps during copulation
how graceful the boy's laugh
in his passion, boys surf the waves

But between them and me the wall

My monkish self is now wrapped in carnality
the aging and love-barren
is now a pitiful peeping tom an eavesdropper
touching fire with his bare hands

But the soul won't be crushed easily
soon within days
the boy has become my love
                    and the girl my beloved
soon within days
I'd wait with a delight free of anguish
for their long soft lovemaking
for lustful chirps in lilac nights
for their conversations rustling like candy wrapper
at times sleep eluded me as I awaited their intimate moments
and in their absence—
sometimes they traveled abroad
or to relatives in Netanya—
my solitude grew and I felt abandoned

And the youthful horniness
that gripped me like a fever
gave birth to despair and want
from which hope and plenty were born
as dreams swelled with futures
and a thing became present as a mount and a river
and from their unions poetry was born

Blue Head

For a moment I was startled—
could it be that from my desert vacation
nothing remained in my head
except for the vision of the boys
who served our meals and cleaned our rooms—
which would mean that nothing interests me anymore
except youth
and absolute simplicity

But another thing captured me too
the blue surface of a quivering sea
I gazed at for many hours

What is the quivering aquatic blue
What quivers in the quivering blue
What is the blue
that the desert mountains encircle

Is it from the blue
that the violet night broke through
as well as the black mountains
and the gliding somnambulist moon
while the border between firmament and water
seemed lost for good

The Sinai Desert Flies

I decided:
the poem about the flies would not be written

But the unwritten poem
flutters at my ear my nose my eyes
settles in my palms

A buzzing pest—hungry to be written

But I decided
the poem about the flies would not be written

I'll only say this and in their praise:
after a million years of evolution
the only species left
are those difficult to catch
those that easily elude a murderous hand

And I'll sing my praises as well
for despite their evolutionary sophistication
I terminated in one blow
two desert flies

And the guilt I feel for ending
the buzz of their lives
I'll defer to another poem

And the matter concerning the black holes
droning on in my head
I'll defer to another poem

A Lone Tourist

In the yellow light of dusk
in a small café in the square
as I pampered myself with tea and cake
among locals and tourists
sipping and chewing like me
there came a tiny brown bird
and asked for crumbs of my cake

I seemed kind and benevolent to her
someone who would not capture and slaughter
or imprison a songbird in a cage

I placed a crumb before her
and she glanced around her fretfully
gave out two tweets
hopped and snatched with her beak
and swiftly flew away to hidden goslings
and then returned to ask for more crumbs
since the goslings loved my cake

Finally she hopped onto my hand
picked a crumb for herself
chewed and swallowed and flew away tweeting
to view from a windowsill
the cakes and the events at the café

After the bird there came a small dog
and asked from my hand strokes and pats
and perhaps even a piece of cake
he looked like a small yellow fox
and I called him Billy as was written on his tag
and after the caresses and the whispers and a few noisy licks
he sat down panting at my feet
as if he had found a new and a worthy master
who morning and evening ponders compassion
and whose cake is a walnut cake

In my fancy I had become Franciscus lite

But later in the evening in another café
there came hysterical and buzzing mosquitoes
seeking to quench their thirst with my blood
as if they too had faith in my rising compassion
but my readiness to let them share my blood
and go mad from itching and scratching
was limited
and I tried to whack the living soul out of them
(if it can be said that mosquitoes have a soul)
and even managed to murder two
and from the rest I fled to my room

In bed I recalled Tibetan holy men:
one gave his body to a hungry tigress
so she could feed her cubs
and another asked to be reborn in hell
so he could assist the suffering sinners

Hair

At night, when all the shops had already closed, I saw at the door of a hair salon a heap of hair that had been left there. That's the hair of my wife, I thought.

Putsina

In whose mind the notion of our marriage first appeared—in mine or Putsina's—I'll never know. But it is nearly certain that Putsina believes she is married to me. Coiled and asleep on the sun-drenched grass, she opens yellow eyes when I say, Putsina. Now a muffled calm beats in her body, after being chased for many nights by all the neighborhood males. When she got pregnant her passion subsided and now she proffers me her kittens on the warm bright grass of our yard. As an avowed bachelor I praise in my heart her discernment that I am not one who could easily rebuff her offer of family life. At any rate, as a spouse she embodies to perfection both loyalty and wantonness.

Role

I have a number of roles
some of them realized
but there are those I don't know
and may never know

I may never know
even my principal role
as my life possibly had been diverted
from its initial track

Among my roles there are a few I favor:
feed the cats on our street
listen to the lament of the wretched
discuss the mysteries of the soul
seek and practice truth

But above all I'm compelled
to look at trees
I must see them all

And not because the cross is made of trees
and not because they hold my beloved fire
and not because, as a child,
I built my first private home
in the heart of a ficus tree
I'm not even a tree advocate

Perhaps it is simply the duty of love
for life between earth and sky
in the nothing that precedes words
a nothing of no purpose or meaning
and no need to go anywhere

from

Book of Ask

(1997)

Another Poet

Her poems were bronzed kids
who rose each morning to a roll and raspberry juice
and then rushed to their shrieking monkey games
at the edge of a radioactive sea
and, upon return, demanded lengthy hugs
having a hard time falling asleep
as if drained of all love from so much play

Mornings they rose again to the raspberry
and to the red-tart word
morning they went back to the roll
and to the crisp bitten word

They had outsized words, fleshy
and words deep as the sea
words radiating like radioactive atoms
whirling words

Friendly Dragon

All that I saw were flitting shadows
most of the time background events kept coming
forms were postponed for other moments
more and more forms were postponed
until they vanished in the sequence of backdrops

All that I did not see this morning surfaced on its own—
the dreams, the I pining for its prospects,
the remnants of yesterday, lust outwitting its fences,
fragments of other worlds,
the sheets from which I emerged,
the golden arc of piss,
the water I bought from City Hall to wash my face,
the toothpaste that neutralizes the sense of taste,
the fire, fire boiling water for the Brazilian fruit-powder,
the fire, the old perpetual fire that will consume the entire world,
the garments, the garments of disguise, the face, the deceitful face,
the face fated to its owner,
no one will see my face,
the driving I that leads my face,
the I who participates in civilization,
the two bonsai trees you must place in the sun,
the tiny statue of the meditating person,
the cashier at the cafeteria collecting the price of coffee,
I didn't even see the light of morning,
I was in the light but didn't see it,
only now I see the pen, I wrote, write, will write

And I'm surprised I saw the pale postal clerk
who sold me stamps and envelopes,
and I felt for her, her excessive efforts to please,
her doubts about her looks
(am I being too coy,
too incredulous?
Am I mirrored now
in all that is visible?)

And there are things that do not surface
but are tossed somewhere like TV newscasts
that grow old the instant they're broadcast
fading in the gutters of sight—

The masses starving in Somalia,
the defeated boxer, the plane-crash survivors, the farmers on strike,
the floods, the earthquakes, the fires,
the man who murdered his wife and daughter with an ax,
who by fire, by sword, by famine, by plague,
the man traversing Niagara Falls across a rope

It seems therefore that I seek to see
it seems therefore that poetry opens like an eyeball
burns in a blue fire
seductive like a friendly dragon

Holy Ground

For whom was intended the new sign
"holy ground"
posted at the Muslim graveyard
that final parking lot
overlooking the sea among the towering hotels

Is the sign designed to deter lovers
not yet afraid of death and its dead
and who make out on tombs
saturate stones with salacious juices
moan and chirp at the edge of the abyss
camouflaged by bushes and undergrowth

Or perhaps it's a sign for the Jews
the deeds of living Muslims
having increased their hatred
to offer a Muslim skull or even a skeletal hand
as a plaything for a child
who will grow up to be a doctor or a pathologist

Or perhaps the sign was meant precisely for the dead
who are not to desire earthly desires
who are not to return nightly from hell or heaven
through tunnels dug from their graves
to share in the joy of those
necking on tombstones

The meeting ground between love and death
is a particularly holy one
since a poet like me
who again was abandoned yesterday
who may be likened to a compulsive Orpheus
always pursuing a missing bride
toward the hell of her rejection
toward his death within hers
and finally returns
at his side nothing but poems
sparkling fresh like dewy leaves

Dolinger

When the neighbors opened their door
whom did they open the door for
for whom did they wait in their rooms
and why did they leave the door unguarded?

When the neighbors opened their door
Dolinger sneaked into their home
and settled there without their noticing
and so lived in their rooms seeing and unseen

At times he stood at the dining table
silent and translucent and watched them eat
at times he watched with them
silly games and soaps on TV

At times like a curious visitor from another planet
he listened to their barking biting quarrels
at times he sat on the terrace without them
looking at the sky and at the great mulberry tree
nights he slept in the living room or on the windowsill

You must be wondering who is this Dolinger
and why he chose to reside with my neighbors
and why a door that opened by chance decided his fate for many days?

Well, this Dolinger grew to hate
the life of a single poet
favoring instead the sweet stench of my neighbors' apartment
whose essence is a synthetic orchid spray

Over the bachelor's poems Dolinger preferred
coitus kindled by scant desire
electronic gadgets collecting in the kitchen
defrosted Chinese dinners
eaten quickly in front of a flickering rectangle
as Amsterdam burnt at its edges
as Somalis starved to death
as diseased Indians lay dying among cows and rats
as Croatian women were raped by the thousands
as nipples swelled like ripened figs
upon beds of soft porn
as a woman in a bathing suit and high heels
stepped between boxers to display the number 8
as the picture of a kidnapped girl was shown
as interrogators dipped the interrogated in baths of excrement
as the everyday kept bending to the rule of the remote control
as the actual dissolved into a dream from which no one awakes

It's possible he simply grew tired of being alone
yet it's possible that Dolinger is a poet
of a poetics different from mine
whose main subject is the life of my neighbors
the life of obsolete automatons
the vassals of words others voiced
hermetic monads always distancing themselves into nearness
beyond the field beyond the fire far from the voice of Aeschylus

Book

When I published a book I sought of course to publicize myself
so that everyone would say here comes Geldman the Poet

As a poet and especially as Geldman the Poet
I have a few coddling freedoms
I don't think about money and power
I'm allowed to be alone and sit idle
or even wander aimlessly
at times contemplate at length the shrubbery
or the look of the sea after sunset
or the birds bathing in the sand
and I sleep when I want to
and eat when I want to
when all will be saying here comes Geldman the Poet
it'll be easier for me to enjoy these freedoms
and to avoid the infidelity
of eyeing other identities

Yet the fixity of a certain identity
in the eyes of others
is also a kind of enslavement
fitting the novice and innocent poet
because the best of poetry is always
outside the poetry circle
outside the defined identity
above and below the poetic
and of course at its margins

But when I published my book
when I made this ordinary gesture
seeking attention and recognition
from people whose poetic knowledge is narrow and partial
especially so with my poetry
I also sought to publicize the poet
in other words make him an ordinary function
in the souls of others
after all poetry connects its readers
to the poet in them
to the sleeping or expiring person
not allowed to appear in public
and so discredit the masquerade
most people are loyal to
as if it were their true face their preferred self

After all poetry connects its readers
to the sleeping person
                                        who upon waking
will dance the dance of asking

Opportunity

Opportunity began to show
its blinking signs began to slow
the inner hidden haste
charting a process
encouraging manners, dissolving fright

It is not a financial opportunity
and not a wide-ranging one
not strawberry fields oil fields or riddle solving
not a finger pointing to the center
not a holdup of the force consuming roses and frogs

But a hazy opportunity
for a moment of clemency
a moment of grace and mercy
for having listened to myself excessively
for my undue loyalty to myself
for inviting danger rather than relenting
for insisting on freedom unattainable anyway
for choosing solitude over friendship
for playing with the wonders of the void
                              and deriding all fullness
for seeking to know more than is wise
for being defiant and insolent rather than modest and diffident
for tending to speechify rather than chat

All of which are evidence of an inflated self-importance
of too puny a readiness to love and be loved
of favoring strict justice over compassion
of a flawed distinction between opportunity and peril

But it can't be said I understood nothing
and, I believe, most of my poems cannot be written off
I've eased the suffering of quite a few sufferers
and with a healthy diet and sports have delayed my demise
I've ridden myself of most of the nonsense
others are still buried under

And there were lovely evenings when I walked as if drugged
in deep and aromatic lilac
and night came quivering like notes from a reedy flute
rousing my skin with pinpricks of yearning
and for moments I touched beauty itself
for moments I possessed it
for moments I even locked it within

And now opportunity is taking shape
having entered a patient course of leniency
and soon a general clemency will be declared
before the crucifixion and not after
a lighthearted idealization
an interpretation entirely in my favor

I Won't Travel This Summer

I won't travel this summer
I feel no longing for a tourist's life
I prefer the feel of a book's
page, a leisurely walk in my neighborhood, ruminations

A languid summer revealed to me
that what's near is replete with distances
I have yet to explore
attractions shaped like rivers and mountain ranges
enveloped in morning fog

In Milano Square* not in Milano
I notice through the car window
a tree shading green grass
a tree a shadow upon sparkling grass
and startled and dream-like
as if it's my very first time in this neighborhood
in a dream divining my travels
realizing I must hurry and visit it
to watch its vital force
as it grows and becomes its complete essence
even place offerings of dew in flower bowls
to offer shade from the intense light
in my feverish steamy city of hollow blue
anxiously anticipating Muslim suicides

---

* A square in Tel Aviv named for Milan.

I don't know if I'll have the time
so many journeys are inviting
to every near distance
to everything the eye glides over
                                        seeing not seeing
perhaps tomorrow I'll see my room
and sail across its revealed vastness
into closets where testimonials about my past have accumulated
into drawers that have developed a life of their own
to the pile of exiled papers
I may write a travelogue
about my eye movement in the kitchen
about the agile lizards
that are diminutive dinosaurs
and about the various red and black ants
that turn my crumbs into loaves

And I'll write a paper about the lamb and the slaughter
about the seven cereals stilled in the jars
about health angels made of soy
about the piggish gluttonous mouth
about the denial the vomit and the abstinence
about the food always lacking
about the food that starves you
about food for the soul and food for the body
about the lost breast and the absent god
and also about the pigeons cooing in the window
screwing and screwing with no restraint no shame

Abused Neighbor

A neighbor, her face creased with lines,
who lives below me in a crowded flat
fell in love with me I believe
because of two accidental hints

They were hinted she thought
in the jeans that dropped
twice from my clothesline onto hers
stretched below and parallel to mine
for she perceived desire
in their yielding to gravity
a perception that rose in her eyes
in our fleeting encounters on the stairs

Clearly if her husband on every occasion
hadn't listed her flaws
hadn't crammed them in the neighbors' ears
precisely on hushed Sabbath mornings
and if her face hadn't been creased
by the prison of her life and its warden
to the point where she was completely
cut off from the passion of suitors
she wouldn't have perceived in the jeans
hints of love and pleasure with the neighbor
upstairs, namely me

It is also clear that were my life replete with love
the neighbor wouldn't have entered the poem

Yes

The sparrow that collected a piece of cellophane
apparently prefers a plastic nest
and so progress is borne on a bird's wing

And I gather a nesting sparrow
into my brain beset with nest yearnings
into my nesting* brain I gather
from the street an expert bird

Buying furniture, organizing the closets,
plastering the kitchen, arranging the photographs in the album,
all these past activities
as with the sparrow
were nesting tactics

Yet lacking a real mate of either sex
I deserve to be reproved for yielding to delusions
still it is possible that the soul knows its mate
is already approaching
his stride heard in the mountains the towns the clear spring skies
in the earthly and heavenly media
an undeciphered message has already been received
even if the intellect still laments

---

* Also means: 'lamenting.'

My Death 1

Many maidens in white dresses
carried the urns of my ashes
black shining urns
bearing an engraving of a frog

And I was astonished
that my medium-size corpse
had generated ashes for so many girls
had my body grown ahead of death
to size extra-extra-large
as a metaphor to last-minute arrogance?

My Death 2

I watched my death
or actually the funeral

The orchestra stood in a large grave
a kind of common grave
or the orchestra pit of the opera
and played something heavy, even dreary

It was a string orchestra
that played without a conductor
in the playing pit no one led

When the music is over, I reflected,
the players must be covered with sand
for choosing to play such a terrible piece
and playing it badly

Meantime I drifted into restfulness
but two girls in saris
poured into my warm grave
green water teeming with frogs

This is not a Jewish burial, I thought,
this is not my final grave
therefore this is not my last death
the hour of my salvation hasn't come yet

Waste

While longing for Nature
while longing for my reticent nature
while worshipping the idol frog
that invaded my poetry like a dybbuk
I suddenly succumbed to culture's demands
and since morning became a compulsive consumer:
morning coffee and cake at Milano Square: 20 shekels
lunch at City Hall Square: 25 shekels
later a book of Zen discussions: 43 shekels
and after that a gray T-shirt: 40 shekels
and in addition a few more minor purchases
as if I were a prominent citizen of the waste culture
but in my praise let it be said
that the Zen discussions were added to my assets
because of a longing for the poetry of Ryokan
who possessed throughout his life
one bowl one shirt one hut
his sole purpose to write poems
about the views of mountain and forest
about the hidden thundering sound of such-ness

And the frog too I did not betray
for in the yellow book of discussions
there were twenty inky frogs made of lines

So it may be said in my praise that I squandered cash and earned a poem
so it may be said in my praise that I praised myself several times
enough

From the cycle "Summer Sequence"*

1.

Another poet was of summer—
summers he returned from blind distances
when the self flees from itself into itself
choosing a slack summery idleness
a wandering nomad in a glittering sweltering city
as if he were the poet Ryōkan
as if he wandered solitary in a Japanese forest
as if from afar a yellow rare emptiness were offered him
and the idleness and the wandering the fire and the emptiness
spawned in him a refined blend
a such-ness as great as mountains
a round dazzling fruit

2. KOANS

When will we hold hands?

Is there awareness in the roses of awareness?
Are there roses?

The night's skies mirror a hidden darkness

Is desire the I?
Is there an I that is not desire?
Is there an I that is my I?

---

* A cycle of eleven parts.

Who am I—I am who

I am one—one desire one want you are one

Please God give me love

3.

A yellow book filled with inky frogs

4.

The red-crested Poinciana
are a present from tropical kings
and the teeming blue night
is a wedding gift from Arabian kings
the slender moon they packed in silk paper
and the fragile glass stars
they placed in padded boxes

5.

How did we arrive here
and how much labor and sweat
to arrive here
and yet we don't even know
if indeed we arrived here
or where we arrived
and is this our place
and how did we arrive where we did
is this the place our soul sought
is this where we intended to be
is the sun's roaring arrogance the sum of our reward?

Almost Flowers

I almost brought flowers, you said
and I thanked you
with humility and joy
for almost flowers
would be flowers blossoming in our fancy
in the thirsting flowerbed of my soul and yours
flowers from a field not a shop
budding tiny and quivering in the spring's breeze
white blossoms with dewy leaves
awaking in our hearts a new virginity
an innocent touch, struck and drugged with the wonder of our lust
and also blossoms of angels' trumpets
will soar in the skies of our love
and peach blossoms translucently pink
will drop through the night upon our bed
and with them almond blossoms dizzy happy and pure
and paper flowers where we signed our names again and again
will adorn our joint grave
already visible through the mist of our future
in a plot suffused with violets

from *Eye*

(1993)

The Last Interview

Prelude:
This is an interview with a dying poet
this is perhaps the ultimate one
yellow frail and ailing the poet drowns
in his stark-white sickbed
Q: What are you recalling now?
A: Cities and boys
Q: Which cities?
A: The cities within the cities
the cities from which the cities were born
the cities in the morning as people awake
the cities that produce dead for the graves
and the leprous scarred and stinking suburbs
that cultivate trash prostitution and sobs
hinterland cities bottom cities cities of pus
cities awaiting destruction from distant galaxies
Q: And what boys?
A: The boys I could have been
the youth I could have contained
the youth I could have burned
the surfer boys going home barefoot
the biker boys in leathers and chains
the dolled-up disco boys and their dyed hair
the messenger boys in their yellow coats
the Arab construction workers splattered with plaster
Q: You sound sentimental and homosexual
A: This is not an election speech
this is a text that puts aside the praise of girls
in favor of other things other deaths

Q: And what are you recalling now?
A: Gardens
night gardens under blinding lights
staged bushes trees of light artificial suns
sparkling grassy stages for the lone rabbit of doubt
and innocent morning gardens sprinkler-sprayed
where a black man practices his trumpet
and mothers adjusting the speed of the swing
the spinning of the merry-go-round
interpreting childhood for their kids
and the mazes of growth between palace and lake
love corners marble models ridiculous mythologies
and the tired gardeners in the fluttering shade
and arid gardens for wind trees
gardens of sand and stone set up by head-shaved monks
sand flowerbeds around rock formations
Q: And where from here?
A: A garden of steps and a thousand fountains
a labyrinth of jets and shards of light
from the jaws of imps beasts heroes and goddesses
a garden where strollers speak Italian
Q: Are you alluding to the Gardens of Tivoli?
A: No. To the gardens within the Gardens of Tivoli
Q: And now?
A: Now I'm fading
a curtain rises before gilded galleries
and on the stage the death of lovers
is a song for a last voice
the soprano drowns in her heights
the tenor drowns in the galleries in the ceiling
a woman as a perfect voice
a man as a symmetrical jet in the air of the theater

Q: We're in Italy again!
A: From Italy we'll sail to Greece
marble statues in blinding light
Apollo showering in the light of mountains
lizards in cracks of stark-white temples
and the muses with whom his loves materialize
bear his children in the shade of woods
Q: Anything Israeli?
A: Here comes the Palestrina Pièta
Q: Really, how about something Israeli?
A: A branching tree in sultry Jerusalem
in its shade a clear cool stone
a stone for the wanderer of light
a stone for summer's rest
Q: That's it?
A: The Valley of Beit Netofa in bluish mist
and the distant Kinneret amid velvet peaks
Q: Anything else?
A: The Issim caves near the lake of death*
alien so alien

---

* The Dead Sea.

Line

I draw a line

What's at the end of the line—
a house, an insect, or a black hand?
And what's in the line itself—
a mountainous road or a dark tunnel,
an octopus' artery or an ink sample?
And maybe the poem—
a starting point reaching for the end point
the winding line between two points
an ascending graph outlining the depths of its descent?

Bomb

Suddenly with no warning or sirens blaring
a long and piercing whistle was heard
and at the end of the whistle a bomb
that fell on my building with a deafening din
yielding the space of its flats to the general void

When stillness descended and the dust settled
I realized I was left without relatives and possessions
a black Seiko watch sat on my wrist
the wallet in my pocket held a credit card
and the light clothes on my body were suitable for summer
now beginning in the land

I searched a bit among the ruins
and found a few photographs of the neighbors' son a basketball player
a girl's strawberry-imprinted underwear
an album of cantorial music, dusty plates
and a small squashed dog that looked like a sock
and through the tears gathering in my eyes
I saw that the entire city was a heap of stones

Glum yet nimble
I set out to find an empty field
I said: This is the hour of the field
sit in a field and listen to the wind
the wind comes from four corners
no walls to block it

the field speaks with the rustle of wind
allowing the wanderer a heart and place
and in the blue starred nights
you will sleep in murmuring groves
and examine in the depth of your dream
the thing into which you discharged such a destructive blow
and was it logically or ethically justified

Nocturnes

The advantage of solitude
the advantage of solitude that slowly becomes apparent
when nights you make your bed
at the foot of the blue mountain
and listen to the rustle of tiger and deer
cautiously approaching the water

*

The advantage of the empty night
over a night of copulation and fertility
the advantage of a night devoid of the lust to procreate
and is free of that mountain
that doesn't know its name
the advantage of a night that grants want

*

From an empty and two-dimensional night
comes the rower in his long canoe
his oar splashes in the murky river
together-together the rower the oar the canoe
together-together in the echoing vastness
its aim resolute but secret

*

The blue of night burns
touched with symbols
upon a skull moon
golden crickets sing
and in the depths of dark foliage
angel trumpets shoot up
moist scents suggesting life

The Ceiling's Looking Glass

Beyond the houses of the dead
who reside in a valley of eternal grass
under tiny tombs and vases of tropical flowers
stands the house of the Buddha

A canal of greenish water
teeming with fattened gold fish
encircles the Buddha's temple
and peacocks squat on its balconies' ledges

The Buddha is large and fat lacking nothing
he's as calm as the valley and the houses of the dead
his mustache coiled as in a child's drawing

The Buddha's guard is elderly
and when pilgrims arrive he works his magic
places a crumb in a child's palm
and whistles for the hungry birds
who hurry from the foliage of the temple's yards
to the offering of bread
"Wish to see your sister?"
he tempts a female tourist
and turns her face up toward the ceiling
toward a round looking glass
in the small looking glass her heavenly sister
the reflection of her lofty face

Outside in the souvenirs shop
one buys crumbs for the fish in the canal
and when the fattened gold-striped fish
dart open-mouthed open-hunger
seemingly kissing under the wood bridge
the quick birds come
to snatch the fish's scraps

Behold and observe the sight:
Nature is hungry, the Buddha is sated

Porn 6*

There was a scar across his thigh
but the rest of him was perfect to the extent
that even a gesture of his hand
was etched in memory a long time
they didn't film his feet
but the often concealed member
was magnified gigantically
luminous and intoxicated in its motion

One assumes he got the scar in a knife-fight
or in a car accident driving recklessly
but his beauty accorded him a calm
touching the women with distance and power lust and boredom

No doubt—a dangerous character
yet his greater danger lay in his enslaving beauty
a beauty deeper than the exactitude of his body
a beauty worn like a magical garment

* From the cycle "Porn Poems" (eleven poems).

The Hottentot Venus* (Porn 8)

In what chains they had brought her to Paris
to exhibit the wonder of her great buttocks
we will never know
but a crowd of eager and curious men
paid for the spectacle of her buttocks
for five whole years
if there was any wholesomeness left in the observing and the observed
this too we will never know
what the Negro thought about the men and women of Paris
its virgins its wives its ivory whores
whose buttocks compared to hers were lacking
in weight and adoration
this too we will never know
if she learned enough French to say:
Sir, a black ass is worth gold
Monsieur, un cul noir vaut de l'or
we will never know what she thought
of the mansions of the Louvre, the Luxembourg Gardens,
the bridges of the Seine, or the cathedrals where at great heights
slender naked men were displayed on crosses
or women robed in white and gold
women who got pregnant without passion without copulation
their wombs compassion a temple of grace
their eyes fated to see God
their eyes fated to lament the suffering of their son

---

* Hottentot Venus was the name given to Saartjie Baartman who was brought to Europe from Cape Town in 1810.

but she must have had gold earrings
or earrings of some golden substance
for it is inconceivable that in Paris they would have let her be
without jewels and adornments
and she certainly had tears and a talent for weeping
that occasionally surfaced between one show and the next

And we will never know how she died
was it the city air and cigar smoke that finally got her
or perhaps precisely the cuisine renowned for its delicacy
turned in her blood into a deadly dose of cholesterol
all that we have left of her
is a crumbling piece
or if you will a great misfortune
what remains of the Hottentot Venus
is much less than the Venus of Milo
exhibited broken in the mansion of the Louvre
from the Hottentot Venus a coroner had left us
only her glorious enormous buttocks and her black vagina
whose lips are thicker than the lips of her mouth
as an illustration of a vagina that is a dark vessel
as an illustration of lust that knows no bounds
as an archetypical cunt of all the whores in town
as a black sin lurking in the most pearly of women

Those who may still seek her buttocks
particularly the view of her vagina
may find them in a large preservation jar
kept at the Museum of Man near Trocadéro
in the very same town that worshipped them
it is easy to charge that coroner
with necrophilia racism and misogyny

but harder to credit him
with excessive passion for that Hottentot female
that induced him to conquer the acidity of time
and to confer on what he saw as the best of her
the eminence of an embalmed Pharaoh or a Nefertiti
a gift from the morgue for coming generations
for the French and for all other nations*

* In 2002, the French government finally returned her remains to South Africa.

from *Milano*

(1988)

Café

In Café Milano not in Milano
a Palestinian waiter makes my coffee
he smiles with the dark burning in his eyes
as one who reads my intentions

Pagan soccer fans
listen to a fat blond man
explain various moves on the field
it's evening but he wears purple-tinted glasses

A hidden signal sends everyone away
even the pretty made-up waitresses leave
and in the empty café it's me and a Palestinian waiter

He sees my gaze and I see his eyes

He sees that my gaze is not political

The hidden signal expels me as well

On the way home on one of the balconies
in a darkness that electricity softens
I see shrubbery and roses

Guy with a Beard and a Ponytail

And why was he trapped in my consciousness
a guy with a beard and a ponytail
who pensively gazed into the darkness
at the intersection of Beit Hahayal?

Is he like one standing on a hill
seeing his life before him
as a dimly lit maze
attempting to decode a few passageways?
Or perhaps he stands as if facing an inner intersection
facing a darkness or even a wall?

And the tiny ponytail—
is it a tiny trendy ponytail
or perhaps Mozart's ponytail
or perhaps the ponytail of Captain Cook
sighting a continent in the distance?

Human Engineering

So very flawed
or despairingly troubled because flawed
he coveted only his perfection
at times it was the talents of others
at times their physical fitness the perfect beauty of their body
at times it was their cunning or even simplicity
in contrast to his entanglements
at times it was their pleasant manner a light charm or some harmony
and with the intimation of old age it was their youth
that stirred his passion
barefoot boys returning from the sea
carrying surfing boards

It seemed that the spirit of man
persistently demanded its perfection through him
adding, with hubris, immortality and physical beauty
disregarding the wearing down of his body over time
and the hereditary shortcomings of his physical attributes
as if the constant anguish weren't enough
anguish resulting from various production deficiencies
in that odd and mundane model that had been fine-tuned
over millions of years of human engineering
equally gifted and flawed

Buddha of the Light

One day at the noon peak of his life
as he sat among deer in the lovely shaded garden
the death of things was revealed to him
a rusty shadow spread into his life
like the hinted presence of evening at noon
like the echo of a distant mourning drum
like the sudden shriek of a falcon that dove and disappeared

His life shattered like a looking glass
the inevitability of suffering temporality death,
made the forms hollow and grotesque
the ties and the illusion of consciousness split from matter
matter returned to its formlessness
became a formation of abstracted particles
consciousness was displayed as pampered cognizance
that suddenly recognized that the prettiest of flowers springs from it alone
that when cognizance is gone the flower exists in the dream of void

Days returned to chaos
sunrises seemed like sunsets and sunsets sunrises
in the depths of the horizon an abyss opened
the individual was exposed as subjugated to universal forces
the private human was revealed as death's subject
eternal youth became a species attribute

One day at the noon peak of his life
that distant drum was sounded
summoning him to the absolute from the wreckage of his life

days he sat under the Bodhi tree
seeking in his soul a remedy for his soul
and for all who are the subjects of death

Bit by bit he killed his desire
and before he became a deeper negation of death itself
on the sandy edge of Nirvana's void
the supreme illusions were revealed to him
crystal cities crystal trees and lakes of crystalline water flowers
Buddha regions shimmering in infinite hues of light
illumined in golden beams

To his followers he left regions of the purest illusion
his love for the magic light of precious stones translucent and crystalline
the beautiful road to Nirvana's gate
the great awakening in the great sleep

Paris

On a napkin in Café Stern*
he drew the ellipse of the Paris map
the first small rectangle: the Opera House
and from there, through boulevards, mantras of beauty,
Rivoli, Palais Royal, Notre Dame, the Louvre, Pont Neuf
and so on, and so on,
a reverse journey to Christ's
stations in the path of pleasure in the boulevards of chestnut trees
in the festive garden of life refined and sophisticated

Termites build towering hills
the species of man builds a Paris
erects a dream city
plants a labyrinth garden

---

* A café in Tel Aviv

Time (*fragments from a long meditation about time*)

A clock whose hands move across mighty waterfalls

Cinderella's midnight hour
she takes her leave from the charmed prince
and returns to the kitchen in a chariot of mice
leaving behind in her royal future
a tiny provocative slipper

A clock that at its midnight hour
a slender maiden in a muslin dress
and a pale lad clad in black
emerge from its ticking box
to dance to the tune of a soft tango
that subdues the ticking tick-tock

I split into a reader and a writer
I'm a boy reciting a poem to his mother
my mother responds to my poem
I respond to my poem

A clock whose face is black and blank
a diamond fixed at this midnight hour

Each night I wait for Y to call

The stretch between first date and bodies touching

An Aztec sundial
establishes the time of sacrifice
the moment the knife touches the kingdom's firstborns

Spring

I was conceived in summer
when my parents felt love in between quarrels
I was born in a spring of butterflies and rats
while clean rivers thawed
even as the earth digested a multitudes of corpses

In the windows stood a city in ruins
horrific sights huddled in the streets
refusing to sink in the gutter of oblivion

The devil danced here, they said,
his barking voice still echoed in empty stadiums
the spilled blood soaked the pavements like hieroglyphics

American soldiers with glinting teeth were the messengers of purity
German women famished and sallow copulated with able-bodied blacks
Jews from the camps went back to commerce
and put flesh on their bones

I was a new boy of a race persecuted throughout history
a race whose interpretations of the books that held its essence
concealed the secret of its essence
a race whose weakness sought its death
at the hands of the power-crazed masters

I was a new boy in a city in ruins
and my mother loved me as a hope, a sign, a blue sky,
and my father hugged me as a man hugs his new sword
and the wool and silk and milk were not enough
to dam my feverish weeping

Poplar in the Window

The poplar in the window at my desk
was a friend
her* transformations in light and in season
became for me the beauty and mystery
of the current that flows through everything

But when winter announced its approach
a neighbor discovered the perils of the poplar
worrying she would shatter his window

Practiced Arab gardeners split her open
and carried her broken and bereft
to a pile at the municipal dumpster

Like a shaved vulva the yard was exposed
shamed barren alien

Next morning winter arrived as forecast as if summoned
like a new eager razor-sharp apostle
and hurled itself onto the windowpane
a mighty iron antenna
its hard fingers reaching to outer space

---

* Poplar in Hebrew is a feminine noun.

Leaves

I put leaves in a jar
pale carob leaves
for I feared the beauty of flowers
might stir a painful yearning

acknowledgments

The following poems have appeared in the following publications:

The Kenyon Review: "Abused Neighbor"
Absinthe Literary Review: "Friendly Dragon"; "Holy Ground"
Modern Poetry in Translation: "Signal, Flicker"; "N.B."
Blue Lyra Review: "Chu"
Cider Press Review: "I Dreamt You"
Catalyst (New Zealand): "I Won't Travel This Summer"; "Tattoo"; "The Neurotic's Poem"; "The Body"

Friendly Dragon; Holy Ground; Dolinger; I Won't Travel This Summer; Abused Neighbor; Yes; Almost Flowers; Porn 6; The Hottentot Venus (Porn 8) have previously appeared, in a slightly different form, in *Poets on the Edge: An Anthology of Contemporary Hebrew Poetry,* and are reprinted here with permission from SUNY Press.

This project was made possible, in part, by a Keren Rabinowitz award, Tel Aviv.

about mordechai geldman

Mordechai Geldman was born in Munich in 1946 and arrived in Israel in 1949. The author of fourteen volumes of poetry, five essay collections, and a collection of short stories, he is also a regular contributor to the press as essayist and art critic. The recipient of the Chomsky Award, the Brenner Prize, the Yehuda Amichai Prize for Hebrew Poetry, and the Prime Minister's Prize for Hebrew Writers, his work has been translated and published in English, Arabic, Czech, French, Greek, German, Italian, Polish, Romanian, Serbo-Croatian, Spanish, Japanese, Portuguese, and Vietnamese. In 2010, he received the Bialik Prize in Literature, and his two-volume *Collected Poems: Years I Walked at Your Side* appeared in 2010–11. Geldman lives and works in Tel Aviv.

POETRY VOLUMES PUBLISHED IN HEBREW

Sea Time, Land Time, Schocken, 1970 [Zman Ha-Yam Ve-Zeman Ha-Yabasha]
Bird, Siman Kriah, 1975 [Tzipor]
Window, Hakibbutz Hameuchad, 1980 [Halon]
Poems 1966–1983, Siman Kriah, 1983
Milano, Hakibbutz Hameuchad, 1988 [Milano]
Eye, Siman Kriah, 1993 [Ayin]
Book of Ask, Hakibbutz Hameuchad, 1997 [Sefer Sh`al]
Time, poem by M. Geldman and 9 etchings by Moshe Gershuny, Harel Printers and Publishers, 1997 [Zman]
Oh My Dear Wall, Keshev, 2000 [Oh Kiri Yakiri]
Poem of the Heart, Hakibbutz Hameuchad, 2004 [Shir Ha-Lev]
Tamir`s Poems (under pseudonym Daniel Kassif), Hakibbutz Hameuchad, 2007 [Shirei Tamir]

Years I Walked At Your Side, vol.1,2, Hakibbutz Hameuchad/Bialik Institute, 2010-2011 [Halachti Shanim Le-Tzidcha]
Becoming One, Keshev, 2013 [Torat Ha-Yichud]
Nightline, Keshev, 2015 [Kav Layla]

FICTION

Neighbors and Other Perverts (stories), Hakibbutz Hameuchad, 2014 [Shchenim Ve-Sotim Acherim]

NON-FICTION

Dark Mirror, Hakibbutz Hameuchad, 1995 [Mar`ah Afelah]
Psychoanalytic Literary Criticism, Hakibbutz Hameuchad, 1998 [Sifrut U-Psichoanaliza: Skira Bikortit]
Eats Fire, Drinks Fire: Psychoanalytic Perspectives: On E.A. Poe, U.Z. Greenberg & Shakespeare, Hakibbutz Hameuchad, 2002 [Ochel Esh, Shote Esh]
The True Self and the Self of Truth: Psychoanalytic and Other Perspectives, Hakibbutz Hameuchad, 2006 [Ha-Atzmi Ha-Amiti Ve-Atzmei-Haemet]
In The Silver Mirror: Bianca Eshel Gershuni: Select Works, Hakibbutz Hameuchad, 2007 [Va Ihie Ba-Mar`et Ha-Kesef]

BOOKS IN TRANSLATION

Becoming One
Portuguese: Cascais, Douda Correria, 2015

CRITICAL RESPONSE TO MORDECHAI GELDMAN'S WORK (PARTIAL LIST, EXCERPTS)

"*Years I Walked at Your Side*"—Mordechai Geldman's two new volumes of poems, spanning forty years of his work, reveal a poet at the height of his creative powers, and place him among the great poets of Hebrew poetry. His poems are meditative, sensual, autobiographical; and always the sudden splash of color, surprising in its simplicity, and affecting us deeply."

—Ben Menachem/Ma'Ariv

"Geldman is one of the very few Hebrew poets who have so boldly embraced the sensual while dealing with the materialistic notions of self and universe."

—Yakir ben Moshe/ TimeOut

"Linguistically and rhythmically reserved, Geldman's poems achieve a fine balance between the emotional and experiencing self, and the philosophical/ metaphysical meanings they invoke."

—Maya Bejerano/Moznaim

"Reading Geldman's two volumes of his collected poems, allows the reader to follow the great transformations in the work of one of our most important poets. Those familiar with his work will appreciate the exactness of the title he chose for the collection: "*Years I Walked at Your Side*."

—Daphna Shchori/Israel Today

"Geldman creates a complete and coherent poetic universe, a kind of laboratory where the self investigates itself, its consciousness, and its dialectical relationship with the world. Geldman's poems are direct and uncompromising, taking on the large themes that have been central to philosophy and art from time immemorial."

—Rafi Weichart/Davar

"One of Geldman's poetic characteristics is the arc of his cultural associations and sensibilities, an arc that extends from East to West, and is quite rare in the Israeli literary landscape [. . .] The sensual and cultural richness, the fine musicality, the originality of observation, and the thematic singularity, combine to make Geldman's work an important and beautiful treasure in contemporary Hebrew poetry."

—Rina Litvin

"Geldman possesses remarkable linguistic and creative abilities. His poems exhibit beauty and depth, investigating the private self as well as the universal, while devoid of all prejudice or preconception. The clarity and virtuosity of his language, its musicality, grant a classicist dimension to his natural non-conformism, as he engages the darker corners of human existence."

—Professor Uzi Shavit

about tsipi keller

Tsipi Keller was born in Prague, raised in Tel Aviv, studied in Paris, and now lives in the U.S. Novelist and translator and the author of eleven books, she is the recipient of several literary awards, including National Endowment for the Arts Translation Fellowships, New York Foundation for the Arts Fiction grants, and an Armand G. Erpf Translation Award from Columbia University. Her translations of Hebrew literature have appeared in literary journals and anthologies in the U.S. and Europe, as well as in *The Posen Library of Jewish Culture and Civilization* (Yale University Press, 2012). Her most recent translation collections are: Raquel Chalfi's *Reality Crumbs* (SUNY Press, 2015); Erez Bitton's *You Who Cross My Path* (BOA Editions, 2015); and David Avidan's *Futureman* (Phoneme Media, 2017).

about ruth kartun-blum

Ruth Kartun-Blum formerly headed the Hebrew Literature Department at the Hebrew University of Jerusalem. She is the author of numerous essays, both in Hebrew and in English, and, most recently, of the books *The Sword of the Word: The Binding of Isaac in Israeli Poetry* (Hakibbutz Hameuchad 2013) and *Reflections on Psychotheology in Nathan Zach's Poetry* (Hakibbutz Hameuchad 2009). Her other books include a historical survey of the poetry of Hibbat Zion; a monograph on the poetry of Yokheved Bat-Miriam; two volumes on self-reference in art; and studies on the poetry of Nathan Alterman and Lea Goldberg. Her book, *Profane Scriptures: Reflections on the Dialogue With the Bible in Modern Hebrew Literature* was published by the Hebrew Union College Press in 1999, and, in 2003, HUC, Cincinnati, awarded her Doctor of Humane Letters, honoris causa.

index of titles and first lines

Praise for Mordechai Geldman

"[Geldman's] reach is perhaps not surprising for a psychoanalyst confronted professionally and temperamentally with the inner as well as outer manifestations of human experience. Readers come away with an impression of the poet as *uomo universale*, a genuinely Renaissance personality, conversant with Greek mythology, world and Jewish history, Chinese culture, the fine arts, flora and fauna, and the expanses of literary imagination."

— Stanley F. Chyet and Warren Bargad, *No Sign of Ceasefire: An Anthology of Contemporary Israeli Poetry*

"These are the poems of a wise man, incessantly plagued by epistemological questions."

— *Yedioth Ahronoth*

"Mordechai Geldman's *Years I Walked at Your Side* . . . reveals a poet at the height of his creative powers, and places him among the great poets of Hebrew poetry. His poems are meditative, sensual, autobiographical; and always the sudden splash of color, surprising in its simplicity, and affecting us deeply."

— *Maariv*

"Geldman is one of the very few Hebrew poets who have so boldly embraced the sensual while dealing with the materialistic notions of self and universe."

— *TimeOut*

"Linguistically and rhythmically reserved, Geldman's poems achieve a fine balance between the emotional and experiencing self, and the philosophical/metaphysical meanings they invoke."

— *Moznaim*

"Reading Geldman's *Years I Walked at Your Side* allows the reader to follow the great transformations in the work of one of our most important poets."

— *Israel Today*

"Geldman creates a complete and coherent poetic universe, a kind of laboratory where the self investigates itself, its consciousness, and its dialectical relationship with the world. Geldman's poems are direct and uncompromising, taking on the large themes that have been central to philosophy and art from time immemorial."

— *Davar*

"Geldman possesses remarkable linguistic and creative abilities. His poems exhibit beauty and depth, investigating the private self as well as the universal, while devoid of all prejudice or preconception. The clarity and virtuosity of his language, its musicality, grant a classicist dimension to his natural nonconformism, as he engages the darker corners of human existence."

— Uzi Shavit